IT'S MY TIME

IT'S MY TIME

Understanding College Recruiting and College Placement

James L. Gamble & David L. Angeron

Copyright © 2020 IT'S MY TIME— Understanding College Recruiting and College Placement

By James L. Gamble & David L. Angeron

All rights reserved. No part of this publication may be reproduced, distributed, or transmitted in any form or by any means, including photocopying, recording, or other electronic or mechanical methods, without the prior written permission of the publisher, except in the case of brief quotations embodied in critical reviews and certain other noncommercial uses permitted by copyright law.

ISBN: 978-1-7351627-9-9

John Melvin Publishing
650 Poydras St. Suite 1416
New Orleans, LA 70130

FOREWORD

The baseball community that James Gamble and David Angeron support is excited for *It's My Time: Understanding College Recruiting and College Placement* to hit the bookstores. Through MyTime Sports, Gamble and Angeron have put their twenty-plus years of scouting experience to good use, helping athletes and coaches. Here's what they had to say.

Knowledge

"I built a relationship with James and David at MyTime as a junior college coach and their assistance is even more valuable to me today as a Div I recruiting coordinator. They really understand the needs and processes of colleges and have helped players advance from high school to college as well as college to professional. Their understanding of the details and rules helps players, as well as coaches, navigate the recruiting process."

Brett S., Current Div I Recruiting Coach

Honesty

"I highly recommend MyTime. They're upfront and honest with players and coaches. They'll find you a place to play — but not just any team. They work to find the place that's right for you.

Mason H., Current Div II Head Baseball Coach

Partnership

"Extremely impressed with MyTime Sports and how intentional they are about promoting quality players. They've taken my needs and not only found the right guys but found guys that are genuinely interested in kids of character

who would be great at our institution and in our program. When you can mix talent and character, it's a great recipe for success and MyTime Sports finds those guys."

Addison R., Current Div II Head Coach

There's a lot to know about college recruitment and a lot for every student-athlete to do. *It's My Time: Understanding College Recruiting and College Placement* is one resource everyone can use to identify and leverage strengths, eventually securing the college career that's the perfect fit.

INTRODUCTION

Before you dig into the book, we'd like to share a few tips on how you can best use the content to set yourself up for success.

First, it's important to realize that no matter who's reading this book – the player, the coach, or the parent – the work has to be driven by the student-athlete. There will be many points throughout the book where the athlete is encouraged to connect with their community and family members, explore external resources, and look with others for help, but the athlete has to lead the way and there's no way around it.

Second, every reader will apply this information to their environment in the way it makes the most sense to them. There may be sections of the book that have information you're already familiar with or steps you've already completed. There may be information you have to read a few times to fully understand. All of that is normal because this book is a guide for every student-athlete's unique journey. Don't skip the hard stuff or the things you don't understand – that's probably where you need to spend the most time.

Now that we've shared a bit about how we'd like you to experience the book, let's look at the book design and specific tips for completing each chapter.

1. Have you ever heard of the SQ3R method for studying? If you haven't, here are the details – and we think it's a great approach to used when reading this book!
    a) Survey – skim the reading material so you know what's coming in the chapter.
    b) Question – make notes in the margins where you have questions about the content or information that you

know – even before reading the chapter – you'll want to learn more about.
c) Read – now it's time to read the chapter!
d) Retrieve – summarize what you read in the chapter, either by talking to someone about it or writing the highlights of what you remember.
e) Review – go back through the chapter and answer the questions you identified in the beginning and look for other key points you may want to revisit.
2. At the end of each chapter, there are action items for you to complete. Sometimes it's internet research or a discussion with your family. Other times it may be talking to people in your community. Whether it's a task you complete in one sitting or over a few weeks, don't skip it. The application of what you've learned to your own life is critical.

Picking this book up is an important first step. It demonstrates that you're interested in securing the best possible opportunities for a college career. But it's only the first step, and what will really matter is your commitment to doing the work to be successful.

Here's to your success!

James and David

Authors, *It's My Time: Understanding College Recruiting and College Placement*

MEET THE AUTHORS

David Angeron and James Gamble came together to write *It's My Time: Understanding College Recruiting and College Placement* to provide one more resource for their extensive audience of players, parents, and coaches trying to stand out in the competitive world of college baseball recruitment. Their vast experience recruiting, coaching, and playing the game provides them with the tactical insights every player needs to succeed.

David and James grew up in the same town and played baseball at the same high school. They were both on the 1990 Louisiana State Runner Up Team, Berwick High School. After high school, James went on to play college and then professional baseball. David also played baseball in college and then returned home to become the Head Baseball Coach at their Alma Mater, Berwick High School from 1998-2002.

In 2002, James and David came together again when James offered David his first professional job as the General Manager of the 2002 Pensacola Pelicans. They won the League Championship that year which opened up more professional coaching opportunities for Angeron. In the off-season, he'd work as a scout for James and the Global Scouting Bureau. Since 2008, James and David have been working together to help players advance to college and professional baseball as well as helping college coaches nationwide find quality players for their programs.

Today David owns Mental Master Training and is a Certified Sport Psychology Coach (CSPC) with an M.S. in Healthcare Management. He educates athletes on the mental aspects of achieving excellence in sport. David has over 20 years of experience working with professional, college, high school, and youth athletes. Angeron is known as an excellent motivator and a "players coach". His years of research in sport psychology and learning how to deal with athletes of different personality types has contributed to his success in getting the most out of athletes.

James founded the Global Scouting Bureau in 1998 and has been assisting players in advancing for over 22 years. Global Scouting Bureau has assisted thousands of players professionally and collegiately and has worked in more than 20 countries around the world. In addition to playing, James has served as a GM, Asst GM, Commissioner of Minor Leagues, Minor League Pitching Coach, Scout & has sat on Multiple Boards for Amateur Sports, as well as founded and sold minor league teams in his career.

Angeron and Gamble have brought their experience coaching hundreds of athletes and their families together in one book – chapters designed to help the readers make the best decisions at the right time. Their goal is to help athletes, parents, and coaches understand college recruiting and placement practices, providing the players who are the future of baseball with a clear path to success.

TABLE OF CONTENTS

Chapter 1: Eligibility & Recruiting Rules 1

Chapter 2: Importance of Academics 11

Chapter 3: Keys to Successful Recruiting 21

Chapter 4: Divisions 33

Chapter 5: It's All Measurable 43

Chapter 6: Official & Unofficial Campus Visits 62

Chapter 7: Social Media Can Make or Break Your Scholarship Opportunities 68

Chapter 8: Building Relationships 79

Chapter 9: Maximizing Exposure 87

Chapter 10: Choosing the right camps, showcases, and teams 93

Chapter 11: Myths 103

Chapter 12: Cost of Getting Recruited 109

Chapter 13: DI or Bust 115

Chapter 14: Committing: Early vs Late 119

Chapter 15: Financial Aid 125

Chapter 16: Letter of Intent 131

Chapter 17: Things to Consider When Deciding on a College 135

◆ James L. Gamble & David L. Angeron | viii

CHAPTER 1

Eligibility & Recruiting Rules

Deciding you want to play college baseball is an important first step toward setting yourself up for a successful college experience, and we've written this book to help athletes and their families keep the momentum up – from the decision through to playing on your dream team. Before we get too far into the fun part of college ball, we want to make sure you understand some of the most important rules that make or break a college baseball career. And we want to pay special attention to a few things.

1. **The earlier you start planning for your college baseball career the better.** Specific examples throughout this book will make the reasons why early adoption of good habits is so important, but in a nutshell, the sooner you start making good choices, the easier it will be for you to land the scholarship and college options you want.

2. **Everyone will take a different path.** We aren't going to tell you what you should do. We're going to give you a list – and it's a long list – of things you need to think about and decisions you'll need to make. We've seen a lot of players who have struggled, but we've seen a lot who have succeeded. The difference is in the small choices each player makes every day.

3. **We're going to talk about more than just your work on the field.** Your game is important, but coaches and

recruiters are also looking at your grades, your attitude, your habits, and your commitment to baseball. Be prepared to think about and make changes to every aspect of your life because competing at this level requires nothing less than total commitment.

We'll start by talking about what eligibility refers to, and then introduce you to some terminology just to make sure everyone is on the same page! Then, we'll take a look at some general eligibility considerations so you can dig into researching what you'll need to do to meet your goals.

What is eligibility?
You probably know that eligibility refers to your ability to play baseball. It's a term used across multiple sports and at every level of experience. But what we want you to think about after reading this chapter are the specific eligibility requirements that could potentially affect your success.

To help you consider the many different eligibility requirements, we encourage you to visit the NCAA Eligibility Center through ncaa.org. This is a critical step for every college athlete to take. To play any NCAA college sport and receive a scholarship at the Div I or Div II level, you will need to register, pay a fee, and be cleared by the NCAA.

If you're just beginning to familiarize yourself with the details associated with college-level athletics, you may not be familiar with the NCAA or you may be more familiar with a different division. Know that we'll briefly discuss several other divisions in this book and there is plenty of information online that can get you up to speed on what the NCAA is to the college athlete. Feel free to stop reading now and check out additional information on the organization if needed!

Once you understand the NCAA, you may be wondering what the Eligibility Center is. Simply put, it's the organization within the NCAA that determines the academic eligibility and amateur status for all NCAA Div I and Div II athletes. Your first step as you consider playing baseball at the college level is to get registered.

It's also important to note that the Eligibility Center is also referred to as the Clearinghouse. You'll see and hear people use both terms in your research, so we just wanted you to know they're referring to the same concept.

Eligibility Center Success Tips
Every athlete is going to end up creating an account eventually, so we encourage you to set yours up early. And to make the process as painless as possible, here are a few tips!

- Create your account by the start of your junior year in high school. That way you'll avoid the backlog of athletes trying to get cleared at the end of the year.
- You'll need to have your transcripts and test scores sent by your high school and testing center. You can't submit them on your own! Research that process in advance and your entire application process will be smoother!
- You'll also complete your amateur status questionnaire, so be sure to have any questions about that process answered before submitting your final response.
- After you create your account, you'll need to check your email and then log in to finish your registration process.

The NCAA will only review your academic records and test scores once it has been requested by an NCAA University. It's common for athletes to feel frustrated waiting for their eligibility status to be completed, but if there is a long delay, it is probably because your specific records have not been requested by a coach.

NCAA Eligibility Center Account Details
At the beginning of this chapter, we mentioned that pursuing college athletics would involve more than just your skills as a baseball player and this is your first look at how much coaches want to know about you! When you complete your NCAA Eligibility Center account, you'll cover the following topics:

> About You: This section contains three subsections that ask for students' basic information (Student Name, gender, date of birth, race/ethnicity).
>
> Contact information: Address, Country, City, zip code, email, and phone number
>
> Residency: Verification of countries in which you have lived, including dates that you resided there.

You'll also see a series of questions about your coursework that may seem strange at first – and in some cases, you may not understand why you're being asked for these details! We encourage you to simply answer the questions honestly and don't generate any unnecessary stress in the process. But we also want you to think about how these questions are helping coaches get to know who you are as a person. They are looking to understand the details of you as a whole student coming to the university, not just a potential member of the baseball team. To get an idea of that, they will look back at the coursework you've done.

Your School Coursework: Here you will be asked to list schools that you have attended. In the general coursework section, you will be asked these "yes" or "no" questions about the athlete:

- Have you attended any school OUTSIDE of the United States and U.S. Territories after age 11?
- Have you attended a U.S. Department of Defense school after age 11?
- Have you been homeschooled after age 11?

List of Schools Attended: You will need to list each school the student has attended along with the date began and grade completed.

Where did you attend ninth grade? (State/ Province, City, School, Date that you began school and grades attended at this school.)

Additional Coursework: Students will be required to answer questions about specific courses. If the athlete answers "yes" to any of the 5 questions, they will need to provide specific examples for each.

- Did you ever fail and retake a class?
- Did you ever retake a class to improve a grade?
- Have you ever taken a college course at a junior college, community college, two-year college, or 4-year college?

- Did you ever take summer school at a different location than your U.S. high school? Or Have you ever taken any of the following:

  - Correspondence course- a course completed at your own pace that does not require a teacher's supervision or assistance.
  - Online or internet class.
  - A course where the lesson, assignments, and tests were on the computer.

An additional set of questions will be asked if there needs to be more clarification from your previously answered questions. Questions may include: Have you ever repeated a year of high school or secondary school?

You may have decided to seriously pursue a scholarship and you may feel committed to performing at a high level in every aspect of your life, but coaches hear that every day. What they're looking for is the player that stands out because their history demonstrates their commitment to the sport. If you were a solid C student in your freshman and sophomore year of high school and then started taking your coursework seriously as a junior, coaches have less positive history to look back on and it will be harder for them to see that you are committed. It's not impossible, and there certainly are stories of successful athletes who emerge as an entirely different person late in their high school career, but it is more difficult to get noticed with that background than one that demonstrates a long and steady path of commitment to excellence.

Your Experience Playing Baseball

The most detailed section of your account is about your specific experience playing baseball. The questions will be about teams and clubs that you have been a part of as well as events you have participated in. You do have the option to register for 2 sports, but you will first complete one sport and then enter in information on other sports.

There are 5-8 sections depending on the sport you play, including the introduction, expenses, training expenses, athletics contacts and teams, awards, additional questions, and event registrations. This may feel like an overwhelming amount of information to share, but don't rush through it. You never know what piece of information will be critical in catching a coach's attention.

You will also be asked specifically if you've ever competed in a sports event or training where any part of your expenses was paid for by someone other than your family, your team/club or the sponsor of the event. If your answer is yes, you'll need to provide detailed information about exactly who paid for what.

Athletics Contacts

You will also be asked if you have ever permitted anyone other than a parent, legal guardian or coach to market your skills in your sport. Like the previous questions related to expenses, if you say yes, you'll need to provide a list of details related to the exchange.

- Did you enter into a written or verbal agreement with this individual?
- Did you agree to future representation?
- Did you pay for these services?

Teams & Clubs

You'll have the opportunity to list the teams and clubs you have practiced or played with since turning 14 years old (in addition to the U.S. high school team you've already shared). You'll be asked to provide basic team information like their name and location, league, division/level, a contact name and phone number and/or email address, as well as the start date and end date of the team.

Like some of the previous categories, you'll be asked to disclose fees paid, awards you've won, and to describe your level of participation, so be prepared with as much of the documentation as you can. It can be challenging to recall details like this off the top of your head, so we always encourage athletes and their parents to be ready to look information up as needed.

Recruitment Terms You Should Know
There are a few key terms associated with the recruitment process. Some of these may be familiar to you, but even if they are, take a look at the following definitions provided on ncaa.org. Sometimes we hear small misunderstandings that can turn into bigger issues that could have been avoided if, from the start, everyone was on the same page with terminology!

> *A **contact** happens any time a college coach says more than hello during a face-to-face meeting with a college-bound student-athlete or his or her parents off the college's campus.*
>
> *An **evaluation** happens when a college coach observes a student-athlete practicing or competing.*
>
> *A **verbal commitment** happens when a college-bound student-athlete verbally agrees to play sports for a college before he or she signs or is eligible to sign a National Letter of Intent. The commitment is not binding on the student-athlete or the school and can be made at any time.*

> *When a student-athlete **officially commits** to attend a Division I or II college, he or she signs a **National Letter of Intent**, agreeing to attend that school for one academic year.*
>
> ncaa.org

As we move through more chapters in this book, you're going to hear these terms more and more, so you must have a clear understanding of their meaning early on in this process. We hear athletes and parents mix up these terms, and it can be confusing, so we'll keep reminding you throughout the book of the language associated with pursuing a scholarship and playing college baseball. This will help you not only understand the important conversations you're actively involved in on a deeper level, but it will also allow you to speak intelligently with coaches and recruiters, leaving a memorable and positive impression with them each time you communicate.

What's Next?

Now that you've had a chance to think about eligibility, we'd like you to answer a few questions!

1. Are you eligible to play college baseball? Different divisions (which we'll discuss in future chapters) have different rules but consider the general requirements and identify any areas that may put your eligibility at risk.

2. Assuming you're eligible, can you think of anything you should be aware of that could one day make you ineligible?

(For example, is there a contest prize that, if you were to win, would make you ineligible to play at the college level.)

CHAPTER 2

Importance of Academics

One of the biggest challenges athletes encounter as they work their way toward earning a scholarship to play baseball at their first-choice university is overcoming early mistakes made related to academics. Grades are cumulative, so what you accomplish as a freshman, sophomore, and junior in high school does matter. And an athlete may find they've closed doors unintentionally if their early high school grades were low enough to drag down their overall GPA.

It's also important that every student-athlete understands how each class they're taking affects their GPA and overall eligibility. Later in this chapter, we'll discuss some of the most common core competencies, but these could potentially change over time and they will vary depending on what division you choose to play in. Each athlete also needs to consider each class they've taken and whether any are at a high or low enough level to be counted differently in the GPA calculation. It is a lot to keep track of – especially if you're fortunate enough to begin thinking about this your freshman year of high school, so we have a few questions to get you started.

1. What are my strengths as a student? What classes are the best opportunity for me to bring up and maintain my GPA?

2. What are my weaknesses as a student? What classes are the greatest risk to my GPA?

3. Am I completing any courses that will count for college credit? Am I in any courses that are taking time in my schedule that aren't adding any value to my overall achievements?

The answers to these questions will be different for every student, but more importantly, the action each student takes in response to their answers will be different. An athlete may indicate that math is their greatest strength and decide to take math courses as electives to boost their GPA. That same athlete may determine that courses with a lot of writing are their biggest challenge, so they may look into hiring a writing tutor.

Similarly, the opportunities available through the high school to take advanced classes or extracurricular activities will be different. Before making commitments, sit down with your teachers, guidance counselors, or anyone else who can help you map out a path to academic success.

Who's on my team?
If you're thinking about a college athletic scholarship for baseball, you know enough about teams to understand that no one wins a trophy on their own. Even players in individual sports have team practices, coaches, and a support system that help them be successful. When you think about what it will take for you to be recruited – for you to be a successful college athlete – start by thinking about who's on your success team and how they can support you.

Parents & Family Members – Your family can support your success in a lot of ways. You may think right away about times when they drove you to practice or cheered for you at games. But your family can also help hold you accountable for honoring your commitments at school and even helping around the house. It's your family that can encourage you, help you stay motivated during this journey, and help you develop into a responsible person.

Coaches – Your coaches know the game of baseball and they know you – a powerful combination that can help you be successful if you know how to leverage the relationship. Your coach can help you improve by being honest about the areas that need work, but also by telling you the best way to make those improvements. They've seen a lot of athletes – and there's a good chance they were an athlete themselves and can relate to your challenges and goals. Ask them questions and tell them what you're working toward!

Teammates – Whether you and the other players on your team share similar goals or not, they can still be an incredible resource for you. They have the best chance of sharing the same challenges, are most likely to understand how hard it is to balance school and athletics, and may even be working toward goals similar to your own. Spend time with your teammates that motivate you and encourage you to make good choices that support your goal.

Teachers – You're bound to have teachers you like more than others, but no matter how you feel about them or the subject they teach, they have the same goal you do. If you're struggling in a class, invest a few minutes in sharing the challenges you're having with your teacher. You may be surprised by how many ideas they have that can help you. And if you're doing well in a class, talk to that teacher about what's working well for you! You may be surprised how much you can benefit from investing time in learning about why the classroom, homework, and studying preferences you like are so effective for you.

Your Guidance Counselor – There's a big difference between what a student needs to be successful and what a student-athlete needs to be successful. Your guidance counselor knows what it takes to secure athletic scholarships and, if you're struggling in any area, is the perfect person to connect you with the resources you need to be successful. The trick is that they can only help you if you let them, so communicating your goals and challenges is critical.

Your academic performance is up to you. You're the one who will decide to study when it would be more fun to play video games. You're the one who will choose to ask for help early on because you understand that your grades matter. But you also have a whole team of people cheering you on! They can be a source of important information and inspiration. Don't overlook the many different ways they can help you.

Specific Academic Requirements
Different divisions and schools have different academic requirements, but there are some common requirements. For example, it's safe to assume that you'll need to graduate high

school or complete your GED to be eligible to play college ball! But there are often other requirements that may not be as obvious.

Since everyone who reads this book may be pursuing different divisions and different schools – and some athletes may be pursuing multiple divisions and schools – we can't provide you with a concrete list of what you will need to be academically eligible. However, we do want to provide you with a general list of considerations to help demonstrate what you can expect. To do that, we're going to share one set of requirements.

Once you've narrowed down your list of divisions and schools you're interested in, you'll be able to create a checklist of your own. We encourage you to compile one list of the most rigorous requirements for easy tracking. For example, if you're interested in two schools and one requires a 2.3 GPA and one requires a 2.5 GPA, list 2.5 as your goal. A singular point of focus will be easier for you to manage and by making the higher goal, you've also covered the one that is easier to obtain.

Sample Academic Requirements

- You must graduate high school.
- You must complete 16 approved core courses.
- You must complete 10 core courses before your seventh semester (senior year), including seven in English, math or natural/physical science. Once you begin your seventh semester, you may not repeat or replace any of those 10 courses to improve your core-course GPA.
- You must earn at least a 2.3 GPA in your core courses.
- You must earn an SAT combined score or ACT sum score matching your core-course GPA on the sliding scale

provided, which balances your test score and core-course GPA.

If the sample list of requirements above were listed for the division you'd like to compete in, how would you measure up? What would your next steps be? To get an accurate picture of what you should be aiming for, complete the following steps for each of the schools you're interested in.

1. Visit the websites of the schools you're interested in attending. Search for their admission requirements and write them down – everything from GPA, assessments, and specific coursework that's required.

2. Review the application instructions. This will give you an idea of what's required, including fees, essays, or letters of recommendation.

3. Complete an internet search of the school's graduates! This step is the most fun because it gives you an idea of who has attended each school and can tell you a bit about the campus culture.

For a lot of athletes, this can be an eye-opening experience. A common surprise is that graduating from high school isn't necessarily going to be enough to make you academically eligible – there are specific course requirements, too. There's a good chance your high school curriculum covers them, but it isn't a guarantee. It's up to you to check and make sure.

Another aspect of academic requirements that often surprises people is the GPA calculations for your *core courses*. We tell all of the families we work with one thing: There's a big difference between what a student needs to be successful and what a student-athlete needs to be successful. The number that you see when your grades are reported may technically be your GPA, but for college recruiting, not all of those courses count. Make sure you're also calculating your core-course GPA – especially if you know there is a risk that it may not be high enough to be competitive.

The team of people we talked about earlier is the perfect resource to help you with your academic success! Take these requirements seriously, but don't let them overwhelm you. Ask for help creating your plan and understanding the requirements so that you can focus more of your energy on making great grades.

What if it's too late?

I know we talk a lot about making good choices early on, and we do mean it. Your best chance at a smooth transition into college baseball is a healthy academic record. But we live in the real world and we get that not every talented athlete comes to us early or with a solid plan already in the works! Remember that throughout this we're giving you tips and timelines that are ideal, but what each player is working with will be different. If you're feeling like you're late to the game, consider these ideas.

1. **Ask a trusted professional for help.** If you're concerned about your academic eligibility or your grade in a specific class, there are all kinds of people who can help you identify the best possible solution. Talk to your guidance counselor, coach, or teacher and share your concern. They may be able to explain the requirement in more detail and

you may learn you were worrying for nothing. They may share an idea for a resource that you didn't even know existed. It's human nature to avoid these kinds of situations, but they don't resolve themselves and they only get more challenging with time, so ask for help early.

2. **Make reasonable changes.** Throughout this book, you'll hear us reference goal setting in general and specific techniques like those found in books like *The Compound Effect: Jumpstart your income, your life, your success*. No matter what goals you're setting, we want you to set yourself up to work hard and push your limits, but we don't want you to set yourself up to fail. For example, if you're currently worried about your math grade, don't set the goal of getting a 100% on the test you have tomorrow or bringing your grade up from a C to an A by the end of the week. Setting goals that are so high they're impossible doesn't help you make practical good choices. However, committing to doubling your study time, asking for help, or working with a tutor, are all things you can control and are likely to complete. They will also move you closer to your ultimate goal of an improved grade.

3. **Leverage your natural talents.** It's easy to get so focused on improving the specific areas of weakness we have that we forget to celebrate and leverage the things we're good at. Are you motivated and good at goal setting? That's great – use the motivation and goal setting skills that helped you improve your batting average to boost your math grade. Sometimes we put our lives into silos – school, baseball, friends, and home. But a lot of the skills that have made

you a successful ballplayer can be leveraged to make you successful in other areas.

What's Next?

We're guessing that you feel like you've got some work to do! The following tasks will help you get organized and clarify your goals and the steps you need to take to be successful. We recommend that you complete each of these questions in writing. Thinking about the answers is a great start, but you may be surprised at how much more you uncover when you write the answers out!

1. Who's on your team? Using the content from this chapter, make a list of everyone who supports your success and how they can help you. Be specific and, if possible, list the specific questions they can answer.

2. Choose at least one division and one school your interested in and review their academic eligibility requirements. This process will serve two purposes. First, you'll learn about a school you're interested in. Second, you'll have a chance to practice your research skills!

♦ James L. Gamble & David L. Angeron | 20

CHAPTER 3

Keys to Successful Recruiting

There are hundreds of thousands of high school athletes in the United States and thousands of college coaches who are looking for the right player to fill a specific need they have on their team. Those coaches are good at finding players – and they have help from recruiters. But in this chapter, we're going to talk about what each athlete can do to get noticed by the right coaches at the best schools for your personal and professional goals.

When should I start thinking about recruitment?
Unfortunately, a common mistake we see among talented athletes is a focus on recruitment that begins too late. If you're entering your senior year of high school and are thinking it's time to *start* thinking about what it will take to secure a scholarship, you're way behind. Pieces of your recruitment plan should already be in place when you start your freshman year of high school.

If you're reading this as a sophomore, junior, or senior, should you just give up? Of course not! But it's important to be honest with yourself and know what you're up against. A lot of the work that needs to be done to connect you to the best opportunities takes time to nurture. If you have less time to accomplish some of these goals, you'll need to adjust accordingly.

Where should I start?
Starting the recruitment process can feel overwhelming, but if you work through this book chapter by chapter, you'll set yourself up

for success. Instead of looking at everything you need to and trying to accomplish it all, create a plan and focus on making progress through small, manageable steps.

Write your plan. Your recruitment plan is what's called a "living document." All that means is that it's never complete. You're going to add to it over the next few years, clarifying details, making changes as you accomplish goals, etc. A simple place to start is by getting organized and creating a shell of what information you need to collect and what you need to accomplish. That sets you up to fill in the blanks as you accomplish various goals.

Stay on top of your grades. As we discussed in the previous chapter, grades are important for the student-athlete. But grades get a special call-out here because they are something that requires your constant attention over time. You can't decide to focus on your grades in your senior year and expect to be successful. Your commitment to your grades needs to start early and be maintained throughout your high school career.

Stay informed. Don't look at your parents and coaches to tell you what schools you should be pursuing. They will undoubtedly have suggestions for you, but it is your responsibility to research the schools that interest you and understand what it will take for you to get into those schools. Your team of supporters will help you, but you need to own the research process.

Information Gathering

As you pull together a plan, you may map out goals according to what you understand about the academic and baseball seasons, but in the world of recruiting, there are additional considerations you should know about. The next section lists a few key terms that can help you as you create your plan.

Recruiting Periods

NCAA member schools have adopted rules to create an equitable recruiting environment that promotes student-athlete well-being. The rules define who may be involved in the recruiting process when recruiting may occur and the conditions under which recruiting may be conducted. Recruiting rules seek, as much as possible, to control intrusions into the lives of student-athletes.

What is "recruiting" in this context? You'll find different people use the term to mean different things! But for our purposes in this chapter, we're referring to how the NCAA defines recruiting which is as follows

> *(Recruiting is) any solicitation of prospective student-athletes or their parents by an institutional staff member or by a representative of the institution's athletics interests for the purpose of securing a prospective student-athlete's enrollment and ultimate participation in the institution's intercollegiate athletics program.*

Contact Periods

A contact occurs any time a college coach says more than hello during a face-to-face contact with a college-bound student-athlete or his or her parents off the college's campus. During a contact period, a college coach may have face-to-face contact with college-bound student-athletes or their parents, watch student-athletes compete and visit their high schools, and write or telephone student-athletes or their parents.

Evaluation Period
During an evaluation period, a college coach may watch college-bound student-athletes compete, visit their high schools, and write or telephone student-athletes or their parents. However, a college coach may not have face-to-face contact with college-bound student-athletes or their parents off the college's campus during an evaluation period.

Quiet Period
During a quiet period, a college coach may only have face-to-face contact with college-bound student-athletes or their parents on the college's campus. A coach may not watch student-athletes compete (unless a competition occurs on the college's campus) or visit their high schools. Coaches may write or telephone college-bound student-athletes or their parents during this time.

Dead Period
During a dead period, a college coach may not have face-to-face contact with college-bound student-athletes or their parents and may not watch student-athletes compete or visit their high schools. Coaches may write and telephone student-athletes or their parents during a dead period.

It's important to remember that when you're reaching out to coaches, there are times when they can't respond to you. We hear from frustrated athletes and parents who feel they're being ignored when the coach they've initiated contact with can't respond to their messages. While this is frustrating no matter what the reason, we hope understanding the guidelines the coaches must follow can help everyone understand the communication rules that have to be followed.

Reminder: Official and Unofficial Campus Visits

Any visit to a college campus by a college-bound student-athlete or his or her parents paid for by the college is an official visit. Visits paid for by college-bound student-athletes or their parents are unofficial visits. During an official visit the college can pay for transportation to and from the college for the prospect, lodging and three meals per day for both the prospect and the parent or guardian, as well as reasonable entertainment expenses including a set number of tickets to a home sports event. The only expenses a college-bound student-athlete may receive from a college during an unofficial visit are three tickets to a home sports event.

Your Recruiting Resume

When you begin to implement your plan, you're going to need what's called a "recruiting resume." It is exactly what it sounds like – a summary of your accomplishments, much like what you'd create if you were applying for a job. There are many standard pieces of a recruiting resume and we've outlined them below, but we've also added tips here and there where we've seen athletes make mistakes or shine. Like all of the advice we've shared in this book, we encourage you to focus on how these ideas can best support your goals.

Building your recruiting resume can also be the perfect opportunity for you to identify areas in which you have the potential to grow. If you're filling out a section and you don't feel particularly proud or excited about the content, that is a clue that you should explore ways you could potentially enhance that aspect of your background.

Introduction

Address the resume to the coach receiving it. Coaches prefer personalized emails as opposed to a generic one. If you send a generic resume it is tough for a coach to determine your level of interest in their university- which makes them less likely to respond.

Lead with a summary of your top accomplishments. If, for example, academics are your strong suit, begin with your academic achievements. Highlight things like your grade point average (GPA), standardized test scores (SAT or ACT), honors/AP classes, favorite subjects, and any potential majors you are interested in. Coaches are looking for all-around great students as much as they are seeking athletic talent, so if this is your strength, make sure it shows! The NCAA is increasing its academic standards and team academic performance is now more important so coaches are more motivated than ever to find athletes that will help raise their team's overall academic profile.

The introduction to your resume is a great place for you to put a link to your highlight video. You should upload your highlight film to a video-hosting site like YouTube. Putting the link between the academic and athletic paragraphs is one of the best ways to get a coach to see your video.

Academic Information

On your resume, you will want to include a section under your cover letter with academic-specific information (even if you included a short list of highlights in the introduction). You will need to include:

- High school name and phone number
- Cumulative GPA
- SAT/ACT score (if you've taken them)
- Desired major (if you have one)
- Your Eligibility Center number (if you have one)

This section is also a good place to list any honors or AP classes you have taken.

Contact Information

Include your home address so coaches can send you packets of information about their program and other correspondence and home phone number so they can organize all of your contact information in one place. Include a secondary phone number, like your cell phone, if you have one.

You should also share your parents' or guardians' names since coaches may call your home, but only as an FYI. Coaches will want to talk to you, the athlete, not your parents.

You will want to include your high school and/or club coach's contact information such as phone number and email address. College coaches will often want to speak with your current coaches; sometimes even before they respond to you.

Make a list of everyone whose information you included and be sure to let them know that you included their name and contact information in one or several applications. The last thing you want is for a college coach to reach out to someone to ask about you and have the person say that they weren't expecting the call! This is yet another opportunity for you to demonstrate to the college coach that you are an organized and committed professional.

Team Information

Let coaches know which teams you currently play for, both high school teams and any club or travel teams you may be on.

Events & Results

This is an opportunity to share your recent measurable successes! List any recent events and competitions you participated in and your results for them. If you know your teams' upcoming games or tournaments, you can include them so coaches can look into attending and watching you play in person.

Creating a Recruiting Video

Your recruiting video is an essential part of the recruiting process. College coaches want to see a tape of your game and practice footage so they can get an idea of who you are as a player. This provides them with an opportunity to evaluate you and determine if they see you as a prospective student-athlete before investing the time and money in traveling to see you in person.

The first 60 seconds of your recruiting video will have the biggest impact on college coaches, so make sure it grabs their attention. Try following this formula to get the most out of your video!

1. **Short Introduction.** Introduce yourself by speaking to the camera or by including a title slide. Include your name, contact information, high school, position, and jersey number and color before the video begins. This makes it easy to identify you on the tape.
2. **Spotlight.** Layer a spotlight or shadow on you during play. Coaches need to be able to identify you on tape if they are going to be able to evaluate you as a player. Choose clear, focused game footage so it is easy for them to do so.
3. **Game and Practice Highlights.** Allow the coach to see you in both competition and training, both of which are essential to athlete development.
4. **Brevity.** Keep the video between 3-5 minutes. If coaches want to learn more about you, they might ask for additional video and you can send that at a later date.
5. **Multiple Angles.** Being able to see your technique from different perspectives helps a coach better understand you as a player. And it's more interesting to watch!
6. **Offensive and Defensive Footage.** Remember to include a variety of ways you contribute to your team – not just footage of what you perceive as your biggest strength. Coaches don't have a lot of spare time, so you want to be succinct, but they also want to see as much of what you can do as possible. Make the most of your video!

Keep in mind, most coaches won't view more than two minutes of your video, but if you compile and organize the right content with guidance and advice from recruitment professionals, you can be confident you're sharing footage of the skills they are most interested in seeing.

In a future chapter, we'll talk about social media, how that can be leveraged, and what you should be careful of. In general, we just want to wrap this section up by reminding you that there are a lot of tools at your disposal that can help you put your best foot forward when connecting with coaches. Success starts with a plan and that plan bears fruit when you follow through and make the most of those resources!

What's Next?

Athletes and parents reading this book may find themselves with some, none, or all of the things mentioned in this chapter completed. With that in mind, we encourage you to complete the items on the list below if you haven't yet and if you've already created the items, we encourage you to review them and make updates based on what you've learned after reading this chapter.

1. Update or create a recruitment plan. Remember this is a "living document" and it won't ever be complete. Make sure it's in a format that you can easily add to and modify as accomplish different tasks.
2. Update or create your recruitment resume based on the guidelines listed in this chapter. Provide as much detail as possible and leave yourself a reminder to circle back as needed to make changes. For example, if you haven't taken the SATs yet but you have your test date on the calendar, you can note approximately when you'll have your scores and leave yourself a reminder accordingly.

3. Update or create your recruitment video. Depending on the time of year and the opportunities you have to play, you may be able to add video clips that demonstrate a skill you hadn't captured yet or even swap an old recording for a newer one that more accurately showcases your skills.

♦ James L. Gamble & David L. Angeron | 32

CHAPTER 4

Divisions

If your goal is to play for a Division I school, do you know why? Sometimes when we ask athletes and their families about where they want to play, we're surprised to hear that they are confident they want a Div I school and yet they aren't exactly sure why that is so important! For some athletes, that is the right goal. For other athletes, there may be better options. Our goal for this chapter is to help you understand the different divisions and then determine which ones are the best fit for your goals.

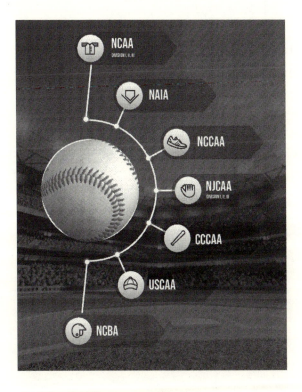

What Level Can You Play in College?

High school baseball is a lot different than college baseball, and the competition is significantly higher in some divisions. You may be a top competitor in high school, but your ranking could be significantly different at the next level. Why does this matter – aren't you always just going to play your hardest? And if you do determine a difference, how does that affect your plan?

If you compete in a league you aren't quite ready for, you may be setting yourself up for failure. Even if it feels like a long path to success, it's a smarter play to go where you know you can work hard and be successful, changing divisions in the future, if that's what's best.

It can be difficult to see what level you're performing at as a player. Especially if you're used to always being a top player on your team, you may not know how you compare to the rest of the country. In a future chapter, we'll talk about a few metrics you can look at that will help, but there are a few other resources at your disposal as well.

Ask Your Coach

Your high school and club coaches can help you determine what level of college sports you should aim for. They are familiar with your skills and abilities and can effectively evaluate your athletic ability. An honest discussion with your coach about where you could play in college will help you find the best opportunity.

Ask an Outsider

Chances are that you'll attend camps or meet recruiters who can provide valuable insight into how you compare to athletes at your level around the country. Ask to speak with coaches and officials about your performance and have them evaluate your skills. This will likely give you a new perspective and a clear picture of what you need to work on.

Consider Your Academics

You'll need a strong academic background as well as strong athletic skills to catch the eye of college coaches, so remember to consider your academic performance when choosing what schools you want to play for. This consideration may rule some schools out for you, but it's better to know early on so you can be clear about your goals. You are attending college to earn a degree while you play sports and you'll need to balance the two. Talk to your guidance counselor or research the admissions requirements for the schools you are interested in.

We've told you that there are different requirements for different divisions and even for the schools within those divisions, and we want you to do research and uncover the specific information you need to be successful. But we also want to provide you with a snapshot of the divisions you are most likely to end up exploring so you can see in one place how they are different.

NCAA Divisions

The NCAA is comprised of three divisions to align like-minded schools in the areas of philosophy, competition, and opportunity. In 2020, Division I was made up of 350 schools, Division II had 310, and Division III was the largest with 438.

NCAA Division I (Div I)

NCAA Division I (Div I) is the highest level of intercollegiate athletics sanctioned by the National Collegiate Athletic Association (NCAA) in the United States. Div I schools include the major collegiate athletic powers, with larger budgets, more elaborate facilities and more athletic scholarships than Divisions II and III as well as many smaller schools committed to the highest level of intercollegiate competition. The facilities are often what attract players to Div I schools, but it's important to remember that where you play and the equipment you have access to is only one piece of your success.

NCAA Division II (Div II)

NCAA Division II (Div II) is an intermediate-level division of competition in the National Collegiate Athletic Association (NCAA). It offers an alternative to both the larger and better-funded Division I and the scholarship-free environment offered in Division III. The NCAA's smaller schools used to be grouped in the College Division. In 1973, the College Division split in two and the College Division members who wanted to offer athletic scholarships or compete against those who did became Division II, while those who chose not to offer athletic scholarships became Division III.

NCAA Division III (Div III)

NCAA Division III (Div III) consists of athletic programs at colleges and universities that choose not to offer athletic scholarships to their student-athletes.

NAIA

The National Association of Intercollegiate Athletics is a college athletics association for small colleges and universities in North America.

NCCAA

The National Christian College Athletic Association (NCCAA) is an association of Christian universities, colleges, and Bible colleges in the United States. Many teams in the NCCAA are also in other athletics associations, including NCAA, NAIA, and ACCA.

NJCAA

The National Junior College Athletic Association (NJCAA), founded in 1938, is the governing association of community college, state college and junior college athletics throughout the United States.

NJCAA Division I

Division I colleges may offer full athletic scholarships, totaling a maximum of tuition, fees, room and board, course-related books, up to $250 in course-required supplies, and transportation costs one time per academic year to and from the college by a direct route.

NJCAA Division II

Division II colleges are limited to awarding tuition, fees, course-related books, and up to $250 in course required supplies.

NJCAA Division III
Division III institutions may provide no athletically related financial assistance. However, NJCAA colleges that do not offer athletic aid may choose to participate at Division I or II levels if they so desire.

California Community College Athletic Association (CCCAA)
The California Community College Athletic Association (CCCAA) is a sports association for community colleges in the U.S. state of California. It oversees 108 athletic programs throughout the state.

United States Collegiate Athletic Association (USCAA)
The United States Collegiate Athletic Association (USCAA) is a national organization for the intercollegiate athletic programs of 81 mostly small colleges, community colleges, and junior colleges, across the United States.

The National Club Baseball Association (NCBA)
The National Club Baseball Association (NCBA) is the national body that governs club baseball at colleges and universities in the United States. Club teams are different from varsity teams in that the school doesn't completely sponsor the teams' expenses and the teams are not eligible to play in the NCAA's College World Series. Many club-sport governing bodies operate as non-profit groups to return the most benefit to member teams.

What does success look like?
We'll talk about common myths we hear later in the book, but we have to mention one of them now. Too often we hear athletes claim that they are playing for a Div I school or they aren't playing at all! A Div I school is a great goal and a fit for some athletes, but it isn't your only option. And just like coaches want to learn about you as a whole person, you should want to learn about all of the opportunities the college you're looking at attending can offer you. Don't close doors to what may best support your future goals because you think Div I is the only place to play.

Other misconceptions we hear are that Div I schools are the only ones that offer baseball scholarships which, even in the brief descriptions earlier in this chapter, you can see isn't true. We've also heard people say that the MLB draft only pulls from Div I schools – also a myth! Albert Pujols, Mark Buehrle, and Tino Martinez are just a few names you might recognize who secured successful major league baseball careers after playing in schools that weren't Division I.

What can you learn from all of this? There's one constant that you need to apply to your baseball career. Learn from history, consider the advice others have to offer, and then make the decision that will best support your success.

How do you choose?
To find the college that will best support your success, you'll have to research more than just their baseball program and your academics. Here is a list of other things for you to think about. Each item will matter to different athletes to different degrees, so we encourage you to think about what each one means to you.

Cost

Most student-athletes who receive a scholarship will only receive a partial scholarship, so there will always be costs to consider. Make sure you understand what those costs look like. You could find yourself equally interested in two schools. Sometimes it's hard to think past graduation, but what you will end up paying for your college is one of those times where it is critical. If one choice means you graduate with significantly less debt, that should make it the clear better option!

Campus Size

Do you want a small school or a large school? Think about how you like your classes to be. If you like small classes with personal attention from a teacher, then you might do better at a smaller school. If you like bigger classes and a larger campus, then maybe you want to go to a large school. You can get a good sense of how you feel about a school's size when you visit a school, so it's a good idea to take a trip to any schools you are seriously considering.

Major/Minor

Do you know what you want to study? Whether you know what you want to major in or you are bouncing between a couple of possible subject areas, this should be one of your main criteria in selecting a school. Make sure the schools you're targeting offer the majors that interest you.

Weather

This may not sound like a big deal, but if you know that you don't want to live in cold temperatures, keep this in mind when you search for schools. Familiarize yourself with each of the regions of the U.S. That way, when you start targeting schools, you won't be surprised by weather conditions that you aren't expecting.

Distance from Home
We all have different relationships and responsibilities tied to our hometown. Are you going to want or need to travel home often? If so, is a distant school a feasible option for you? The opposite may be true – you may be inspired to explore a different part of the country and live independently! However you feel, make sure you calculate how trips home will affect your plan.

What's Next?
We hope this chapter gave you a lot of insight into what matters when considering what division and college you want to play for. Now we'd like you to apply some of these considerations to your own life and answer the questions we've posed.

1. Review the division descriptions listed in this chapter. What did you learn? Did this information change your thinking or approach in any way? Or did it confirm the goals you'd already set?
2. Consider the 5 categories listed at the end of this chapter – cost, campus size, major/minor, weather, and distance from home. Rank them in the order that they are important to you and note any goals you associate with them (i.e., how much debt are you willing to accrue during college, what climates are you willing to live in, etc.)

◆ James L. Gamble & David L. Angeron | 42

CHAPTER 5

It's All Measurable

Oftentimes when we meet with players and their families for the first time, they're looking at investing time, money, and energy into pursuing college scholarships and a professional baseball career because their experience so far has indicated that their athlete has talent. The challenging part of that initial conversation is determining whether the athlete seems more talented than they are simply because of the league they're playing in. In other words, on a team where there aren't any strong players, a mediocre athlete will shine. The opposite is also true. There's a risk truly gifted players could be missed if overshadowed by a one-in-a-million player. That's why we start with five measurements to determine where each athlete is at in comparison to national averages – not just their home team.

MLB Grading Scale
Scouting grades are used to help recruiters, players, and coaches speak the same language. A consistent scale like the one below is used when assessing each of the five measurements covered in this chapter.

GRADE	DEFINITION
80	ELITE
70	WELL ABOVE AVERAGE; PLUS-PLUS
60	ABOVE AVERAGE; PLUS
50	AVERAGE
40	BELOW AVERAGE
30	WELL BELOW AVERAGE
20	POOR

As we share each of the five areas to consider – and then one bonus consideration – we want you to keep in mind that each of these measurements can be improved and all the measurements are part of a bigger picture. In other words, if you don't have the right numbers in one area, commit to a plan to improve that area. And just because you aren't where you need to be for one measurement doesn't mean another area won't make up for it. These are guidelines – the same guidelines scouts are using – and you should view them as your opportunity to use industry insight to your advantage.

The Eyeball Test

Whether you like it or not, important people who will heavily influence your baseball career are going to begin making decisions about your value based on your appearance. Before we get into the measured considerations scouts use, we're going to talk about appearance. The eyeball test is what we call the steps a recruiter instinctively follows in the first five to ten seconds after he sees a player for the first time. Ask yourself the following questions:

- Do I look like a healthy, committed athlete? Am I a healthy weight? Are my height and physical strength comparable to or better than successful athletes my age?
- Does my appearance align with professional baseball standards? Are my tattoos covered? Are my face and ears free of piercings?
- How do I carry myself? Do I seem confident and committed?
- When I meet someone, do I have a strong handshake and make eye contact?
- During the game, am I focused or joking around with teammates?

You may feel frustrated by some of those questions and your gut reaction may be to say, "That's not fair!" And we agree with you – it isn't fair to judge people based on their appearance. But remember: We're telling you how things are and giving you the inside track to getting off on the right foot with a recruiter. You have the power to disregard our advice, but we're sharing it because we know small changes to your appearance can make a huge difference in keeping the attention of the people who will help you be successful. Wherever you are, someone could be watching and small adjustments could make your transition to the next level easier.

Targets

Now that we've covered the opportunities you have to make the perfect first impression by looking like a committed athlete, we're going to explore the five measurements every recruiter cares about and targets you should consider.

- Arm Strength
- Foot Speed
- Raw Power
- Fielding
- Hitting

Each of these measurements is important to different degrees depending on the position being considered – that's why we call it a *target*. You'll likely find target numbers you've already hit and ones you don't feel are even possible. With a little research, you'll also find athletes who are successful at every level who can't hit these targets. It isn't an exact science, but you need a starting point. These metrics will provide you with that.

Your best bet is to know where you're at in every category and make any improvements you think you may need to be competetive. When you read each of the following, think about:

- how you can measure exactly where you're at.
- what you can do to improve your performance (if needed).
- what you need to do to maintain your performance (if you've already achieved the target metric).

Arm Strength

Arm strength is measured by a radar gun that calculates velocity. In fact, some scouts and coaches may refer to this measurement as "arm velocity." The need for each position is different, so there isn't one set number they have in mind, but we've provided you with a few general guidelines. Scouts watch a player throw and decide in their mind whether or not he fits the position they're looking for.

Feedback for pitchers is a little different. Scouts and coaches grade each pitch – fastball, curveball, etc. Which pitches are graded and whether or not deception, arm action, or other considerations are included will vary depending on who's conducting the assessment.

GRADE	FASTBALL VELOCITY
80 ELITE	97 MPH+
70 WELL ABOVE AVERAGE; PLUS-PLUS	94-96 MPH
60 ABOVE AVERAGE; PLUS	92-94 MPH
50 AVERAGE	89-91 MPH
40 BELOW AVERAGE	87-89 MPH
30 WELL BELOW AVERAGE	85-87 MPH
20 POOR	< 84 MPH

Remember that arm strength is only one of the measurements they're looking at. If they see an arm at the speed they need or higher for a shortstop, you've got their attention. If it isn't quite high enough, but they see other traits they like, you may be in the running for second base.

Want to improve your arm strength? Here's what we recommend.

- Work with someone who understands the mechanics of the throwing motion. Most communities have someone who specializes in improving the specific art of throwing and can provide detailed feedback for improvement.
- Common and valuable advice is also to improve your core. With a stronger core, your throwing will improve.
- Practice throwing! Did we even need to say that? The fact is, we tend to do what comes easily. You need to force yourself to focus on the hard stuff sometimes.
- Always track your progress so you can see what's working.

Foot Speed

Foot speed is measured by clocking an athlete running a 60-yard dash. For accuracy, a stopwatch or a laser is used to record the time. Like arm strength, an athlete who registers as a slower runner may not be of interest to the recruiter or they may simply shift to another open position. Catchers, for example, don't need off-the-chart foot speeds.

GRADE	FOOT SPEED: HOME TO 1B (LH HITTER / RH HITTER)
80 ELITE	3.9 SECS / 4.0 SECS
70 WELL ABOVE AVERAGE; PLUS-PLUS	4.0 SECS / 4.1 SECS
60 ABOVE AVERAGE; PLUS	4.1 SECS / 4.2 SECS
50 AVERAGE	4.2 SECS / 4.3 SECS
40 BELOW AVERAGE	4.3 SECS / 4.4 SECS
30 WELL BELOW AVERAGE	4.4 SECS / 4.5 SECS
20 POOR	4.5 SECS / 4.6 SECS

Want to increase your foot speed? Here's what we recommend:

- Start sprinting – that's what will increase your foot speed.
- Like arm strength, tracking your progress is critical. The standard testing distance is 60 yards, so time yourself and keep track of your improvement!
- Find an expert in your community who can assess your form. They may identify a few simple adjustments that will increase your speed.

Raw Power

Raw power is also measured by velocity – which is why you'll hear professionals use the term *exit velocity* when measuring an athlete's performance. Scouts watch for two things when they observe a player: how far did the ball go and how much effort did it take?

They're looking to see if the athlete exerted a lot of energy and whether or not he'd be able to repeat his performance.

GRADE		HIT POWER (HOME RUN POWER)
80	ELITE	39+ HRS
70	WELL ABOVE AVERAGE; PLUS-PLUS	32 - 38 HRS
60	ABOVE AVERAGE; PLUS	35 - 32 HRS
50	AVERAGE	17 - 25 HRS
40	BELOW AVERAGE	11 - 17 HRS
30	WELL BELOW AVERAGE	5 - 11 HRS
20	POOR	< 5 HRS

Want to improve raw power? Here's what we recommend:

- Work with a performance trainer (speed, strength, agility) to improve your overall strength.
- Track your movable size and strength improvements. To be successful, you'll need to be quick and strong.

> **What about the outliers?**
>
> Invariably, athletes we work with will question targets. They will make the very good point that Bo Jackson, Babe Ruth, and Derek Jeter all had measurements that fell outside the listed targets. There are a few reasons for that!
>
> First, remember that these targets are just *targets*. It's not an exact science, but having a goal will help you be successful.
>
> Second, remember that a recruiter is looking at the whole player. There's no expectation that everyone hits every target every time. But again, for your development, you need to have something to shoot for.
>
> And finally, a lot of baseball greats are what we call outliers – people who excel far beyond reasonable expectations and general guidelines. Almost 20,000 people have played Major League Baseball, and yet most people can only name a few players. The people we tend to remember are outliers. They are great for inspiration, but they aren't very helpful for goal setting.

Fielding

There are a lot of statistics that contribute to an athlete's fielding ability percentage or fielding average. Essentially, fielding percentage measures the number of times you correctly handle a batted or thrown ball. This would include putouts and assists (which are good for your average) and errors (which are bad for your average). The formula for calculating your fielding ability is:

$$\frac{\text{Putouts + Assists}}{\text{Opportunities (i.e., Putouts + Assists + Errors)}}$$

For example, a 940 fielding percentage would be below average. That means 940 times out of 1000, the player was able to feel the ball clearly and make a play. The scout is judging the infielder's hands, how soft they are, the positioning of the hand, and overall how well you play the outfield. In addition to the calculation, scouts will ask themselves:

- Does this player cover ground well?
- Does he take good angles to the ball?
- Does he get good reads off of the bat and then get behind the ball and work through it?

Like we covered in the previous categories, there are a lot of times you look at foot speed, arm strength, and fielding all together. A scout may say, "We work with him as a center fielder because he's extremely fast, and he has a really good arm." They may move a player to the right side of the field if they have a below-average arm or the left side of the field if they have a strong arm. Each measurement is important, but they should always be seen as one piece of the bigger picture.

Want to improve your fielding skills? Here's what we recommend:

- Go online and check out new techniques.
- Practice anything that requires hand-eye coordination (dance, juggling, etc.)

- Practice using both hands to complete various skills (dribble a basketball with both hands, throwing and catching a tennis ball with both hands)
- As always, track your progress to see what's working.

Hitting

Hitting ability is considered by many professionals in baseball to be the most important measurement, and it is the one that is the most subjective. Statistics are going to tell a scout what a player did and didn't do, but the statistics themselves need clarification.

At the high school or younger level, recruiters rarely consider statistics because they usually don't transfer – there's no way to know the caliber of the pitcher throwing against the player. There's too much data that's missing to trust the numbers. Instead, a scout uses their professional judgment – their educated opinion. They look at several specific things to determine whether the player can compete at the next level.

- Is the bat flat through the zone?
- Does he have a repeatable swing?
- Can he recognize and respond to a pitch?
- Can he manage his at-bat?
- Does the athlete have a balanced approach to hitting?

Even though the measurement isn't as concrete as the others, there are still consistent things scouts look for. That list can be a great place to start.

GRADE		HIT TOOL
80	ELITE	.320 +
70	WELL ABOVE AVERAGE; PLUS-PLUS	.300 - .320
60	ABOVE AVERAGE; PLUS	.285 - .300
50	AVERAGE	.270 - .285
40	BELOW AVERAGE	.250 - .270
30	WELL BELOW AVERAGE	.225 - .250
20	POOR	< .225

Want to improve your hitting skills? Here's what we recommend:

- Repetition. Spend some time at the batting cage!
- Find a coach that understands the mechanics of a swing. Like foot speed, there could be something simple you can do to improve your game.
- Keep track of what works!

The Compete Tool

The sixth consideration scouts will acknowledge is an intangible – and we call it the Compete Tool. Some people simply have something special about them that makes them a competitor no matter what the odds are. You can't identify that resiliency and commitment to improvement through a metric. You can tell some athletes based on concrete data what they can and can't do, and it won't matter. No matter how far behind they are or how many times they're knocked down, they'll always overachieve.

This intangible is probably the most sought-after tool, but it's impossible to define. To see it, you have to get to know the player. What makes him great is the ability to lack some of the other tools and keep succeeding.

When we look for great players, we don't just want to know what they do at practice. It's what you do outside of practice and between games. How do you do at school? Could you do better if you work hard? Have you accepted being average in school…because that tells me you don't have what it takes to be an above-average performer?

Mental Training

We've seen thousands of physically talented players with solid baseball fundamentals fail to make it past high school baseball. The athletes that do advance to elite levels typically have 4 key characteristics.

Most athletes and their parents spend a lot of time and money focusing on building physical skills (speed, strength, agility, etc.) and baseball fundamentals (pitching lessons, hitting lessons, fielding lessons, etc). Those players look great at practice and in unimportant games, but against higher levels of competition, it becomes obvious that they lack the other 3 characteristics of elite athletes.

Sport psychology and mental training is probably the most important characteristic necessary to compete at an elite level. No matter how strong, fast, or fundamentally sound you are, if you are mentally weak, you will not succeed at the college or professional level. Mental training helps athletes manage nerves, perform under pressure, battle through adversity, play with confidence, embrace failure, and bounce back from injuries.

The athlete's knowledge of the game is another critical component of success. We discuss the importance of academics in this book, but the player's knowledge of the game, or "Baseball IQ," is just as important. We often go to scout players that are very talented physically, but when we see them in a game, it's clear they don't fully understand the rules. They make bad decisions in critical situations, or they don't have good baseball instincts. It is important to be a student of the game.

We've seen players and coaches at every level, and we're still learning! When you stop learning, it's time to get out of the game altogether. Players that are constantly making baserunning mistakes, or don't have good instincts to know what to do with the ball when it's hit to them in certain situations, will never be able to compete at an elite level. The game of baseball speeds up at every level of advancement. A high "Baseball IQ" can help slow the game down and put you in the right place at the right time by understanding the situations like knowing a hitter's tendencies or knowing where to throw the ball if it's hit to you with a runner on 2nd base.

Finally, at the top of the pyramid, you see desire. To play the game at an elite level, you must have a desire or heart for the game. At the college and professional level, the game is not just for fun anymore. It becomes a job. It takes an extreme work ethic, dedication, and character to compete at that level. Many players grow up thinking they have that desire or passion to play college or professional baseball because their parents always paid for and drove them to extra lessons during youth and high school seasons. But when they get out on their own in college, many quickly realize that they don't have the desire to motivate themselves to go and do the extra work on their own. They start to realize that their entire life, they were chasing their parents' dreams and desire to be a college athlete. And many of those players quit after their freshman year.

What's Next?

Scouts walk into a game with a blank sheet of paper for every player they're looking at. There are two reasons they add to your sheet.

- ♦ Do something great. When the scout sees something they like, they'll want to find out who you are. You've caught their attention by the way you look or with something you did.
- ♦ Do something badly. If you're the player that has a bad attitude, bad posture, the bad body language, they also write your number down. It's for a different reason, but you still made an impression.

You don't want to be on the list because of a negative impression – it will just make your journey to success that much more difficult. And now you know what scouts are looking for, you know how to get on the list that will help your career! Next, you have some questions to answer, commitments to make, and work to do.

1. What kind of first impression am I giving? What can I do to strengthen what a scout thinks of me within the first few seconds of seeing me?

   Current state:

   Commitment to improvement:

I will improve by (state a specific and measurable action you can commit to that will help to improve or maintain this skill):

2. What's my arm strength? If it isn't where it needs to be, what can I do to improve? If it is where it needs to be, what do I need to commit to in order to maintain this level of performance?

Current state:

Commitment to improvement:

I will improve by (state a specific and measurable action you can commit to that will help to improve or maintain this skill):

3. What's my foot speed? If it isn't where it needs to be, what can I do to improve? If it is where it needs to be, what do I need to commit to in order to maintain this level of performance?

Current state:

Commitment to improvement:

I will improve by (state a specific and measurable action you can commit to that will help to improve or maintain this skill):

4. What's my exit velocity? If it isn't where it needs to be, what can I do to improve? If it is where it needs to be, what do I need to commit to in order to maintain this level of performance?

Current state:

Commitment to improvement:

I will improve by (state a specific and measurable action you can commit to that will help to improve or maintain this skill):

5. What's my fielding percentage? If it isn't where it needs to be, what can I do to improve? If it is where it needs to be, what do I need to commit to in order to maintain this level of performance?

Current state:

Commitment to improvement:

I will improve by (state a specific and measurable action you can commit to that will help to improve or maintain this skill):

6. What's my hitting ability? If it isn't where it needs to be, what can I do to improve? If it is where it needs to be, what do I need to commit to in order to maintain this level of performance?

Current state:

Commitment to improvement:

I will improve by (state a specific and measurable action you can commit to that will help to improve or maintain this skill):

7. Where would I rank my desire and ability to compete? How resilient am I? What can I commit to doing to improve that resiliency?

Current state:

Commitment to improvement:

I will improve by (state a specific and measurable action you can commit to that will help to improve or maintain this skill):

CHAPTER 6

Official & Unofficial Campus Visits

Eventually, you will get to the point where you are ready to start visiting college campuses! This is an important step in your journey for a few specific reasons.

First, you will learn about schools, their educational programs, and how they support athlete success through online resources and maybe a few phone calls. But when you arrive on campus, your understanding of the school's culture and how you fit into it will be taken to another level. Many students are sure they know where they want to go to college and then – to everyone's surprise – a campus visit to a different school wins them over. It's hard to explain and it's different for everyone, but there's no denying they are important.

Second, there is a good chance this will be an important opportunity for you to make a powerful impression on the coaches and other college staff. You have the opportunity to help them see you as a player they just can't do without. Because of that, we're going to focus on what you can do to make the most of those campus visits.

What are official and unofficial campus visits?
An important place to start discussing campus visits is with the definitions of official and unofficial visits. The distinction is important to understand and NCAA has provided a clear definition.

What is the difference between an official visit and an unofficial visit?

Any visit to a college campus by a college-bound student-athlete or his or her parents paid for by the college is an official visit. Visits paid for by college-bound student-athletes or their parents are unofficial visits.

During an official visit the college can pay for transportation to and from the college for the prospect, lodging and three meals per day for both the prospect and the parent or guardian, as well as reasonable entertainment expenses including three tickets to a home sports event.

The only expenses a college-bound student-athlete may receive from a college during an unofficial visit are three tickets to a home sports event. (ncaa.org[i])

You probably noticed that the key differentiator between official and unofficial visits is who pays for the trip! A student-athlete and their family can go on an unofficial visit to a campus. There are rules about what grade the athlete needs to be in to meet with the coach, so be sure to check the guidelines before reaching out to set up a visit. You may contact a campus too early and the coach may not be able to respond. In those cases, don't take it personally – they have to follow the rules.

It's also a good idea to check the campus calendar before you choose your dates to visit. If you go during homecoming or some other major campus event, you'll run the risk of paying higher hotel prices and having a hard time connecting with college staff. At the same time, you may want to time your visit when you know there's a game you can watch! Whatever your goal, know that events are always posted on the college website, so you can make the perfect plan.

If you are invited for an official visit, that means the coach has done their homework and wants to learn more about you and your family. That is exciting and something to be proud of – but it isn't a guarantee they'll extend a scholarship offer. Just because they want to meet you doesn't mean they've made any decisions yet. That's why this next section is so important for an official or unofficial visit.

Do Your Research
Sometimes when we talk to athletes, they'll tell us how much they like a particular school or that they're interested in a specific team. This is what we want to hear! We love knowing that they're thinking about where they want to play college ball. But sometimes we're surprised to learn that someone who says they're interested in a specific school hasn't done any research about the school and can't even really explain why they like it.

This is problematic for two reasons. The first is that if you can't describe why you're interested in a school, you're probably not interested for the right reasons. Second, if you do connect with a representative from the school, they're going to figure out pretty quickly that your expressed interest never translated to any meaningful research on your part. You risk making a negative first impression if you don't do some research in advance.

When you find a school you're interested in, complete the following steps before any phone interviews or campus visits.

1. Visit their website. You'll be able to quickly see what they promote, what events are happening on campus, and what academic programs they offer. You'll have a sense of the campus culture, too.

2. Search for them in the news. What are they known for? Have their students won any awards or been in the news?

3. Look up information about the coaching staff. Knowing the coach's background and few successes the team has had will help you get to know the coach and give you something to talk about when you meet.

Coaches love to talk about their team, but there's a big difference between a potential recruit who comes in and says, "I'd love to hear about your team" and one that says, "I saw three pitchers you've worked with have gone on to the major leagues. That's what made me want to visit this campus." The first example makes a person look interested, but the second example makes a person look *interesting*.

> **Recommended Reading**
> *The Compound Effect: Jumpstart Your Income, Your Life, Your Success* by Darren Hardy
> Have you noticed that throughout this book we keep returning to small choices you can make again and again over time to get the big results you're looking for? If you like the approach, check out this book. We love it and it has a ton of relevant information for any athlete serious about next-level competition.

What's next?
Campus visits are an important part of your journey, but they're also unique to every player. When you do your research, you may find that the schools you thought you were interested in aren't as appealing as they initially were. You may learn that your first choice isn't interested in you. But eventually you'll find the program you

want to study at a college whose coach is looking for your skillset. To make sure you're set up for success, consider the following questions.

1. What colleges are you interested in learning more about? Be sure to list at least five to start – even if you think you're only interested in one.

2. For each of the colleges listed above, list at least 2-3 reasons why you're interested in learning more about them. Include everything from their baseball and academic programs to the fact that you like the weather in that part of the country. At this point, everything is fair game!

3. For the same list of schools, research the coaching staff and the facility.

4. For the same list of schools, research the current and past players and note their performance metrics.

5. Review your list of schools and ask yourself if your top choice changed – or if it didn't change entirely, are there now a few more schools you're interested in?

6. Review the list of current and past players and note any areas you may need to improve to meet the expectations of the coaches and teams you're interested in.

CHAPTER 7

Social Media Can Make or Break Your Scholarship Opportunities

We've already talked a lot about the opportunities an athlete has to make an impression on recruiters and coaches. But in today's high-tech world, the first impression you make could happen before you've even thought about a specific college or university! With just a few clicks, anyone can access your social media accounts and see what an athlete's been talking about online. Even more surprising to some people is that, because of the interconnectedness of social media accounts, people who aren't even looking for you yet may meet you for the first time. That's why managing your digital presence carefully is so important.

If you're wondering why this chapter isn't titled *Close All of Your Social Media Accounts*, it's because social media can also be leveraged to help you connect with the right people and make the perfect first (or second or third) impression. We don't want anyone to be afraid of how people – athletes, coaches, parents, recruiters – are using social media. We just want everyone to understand the risks and make the most of the opportunities.

The following are a few tips to help you maintain a healthy presence online. Read through each of them and note any that stand out to you. At the end of the chapter, you'll have the opportunity to reflect on how you can apply these techniques.

What are the dangers of social media?

Let's start with what can go wrong! After all, those are the stories you hear most often, aren't they? Recently, Kaplan Test Prep found that 35 percent of admission officers surveyed at 365 colleges said they do check an applicant's social media, such as Facebook, Instagram or Twitter to learn more about them. College and university recruiters certainly follow similar steps before investing time in a potential recruit. Let's take a look at some of the most common mistakes athletes make.

Undesirable behavior

What most parents and coaches talk to student-athletes about is the importance of avoiding parties or activities that are in any way dangerous or illegal. Even if the athlete isn't the one breaking rules, the association alone can cost them a scholarship. Consider how it would look to a recruiter if they found a picture of a potential recruit at a party where it looked like underage drinking was happening. Even if the athlete wasn't drinking and even if it was a misunderstanding and no underage drinking occurred, it's the optics that matter. It's unlikely that a recruiter is going to take the time to ask you to explain the photo. It's much more likely they will just move on to their next candidate.

Tagging

Do your friends know and understand what it means to play college ball? If you spend the majority of your time with the same friends and family, take the time to educate them on how important your digital presence is. And, if you ever find yourself in a situation where someone wants to take a picture of you, but you're concerned the photograph could be perceived negatively, don't be afraid to politely ask to be excluded from the photo. You may even be able to get out of the photo by offering to take the picture – and then you've avoided a potentially damaging situation and helped a friend out!

Bullying & negative comments

We wouldn't ever endorse bullying or leaving negative comments on social media pages – that only hurts other people and harms your reputation. Even negative posts or comments about rival teams should be avoided. Always root *for* your team instead of *against* someone else.

But sometimes friends and even friendly rivals will poke fun at each other online in the spirit of competition. Two challenging aspects of social media related to these instances are the absence of tone in written content and the absence of context for the video. You're inside joke with a teammate about their weight costing them the game last week or a video of your teammates celebrating a victory in a dark parking lot after a game could easily be misconstrued. You have to consider how every post could be interpreted by someone on the outside.

Questionable username or profile information

Similar to bullying and negative comments, your username or content in your profile may not leave recruiters with the impression you want them to have. A name or reference that is perfectly innocent may be perceived negatively to someone who is just getting to know you. Not all nicknames are bad – Alex Rodriguez can go by "A-Rod" because the root of the nickname is obvious. Just ask yourself how people will interpret username and profile content!

These potentially damaging situations may come up more often than you realize. You may find yourself at a family barbecue where all of the adults around you are drinking – but in the photo it's not clear that they are adults, that it's a family event, or that you *aren't* drinking. You may find yourself volunteering at a political campaign which, on the surface, seems like a great way to demonstrate a commitment to your community, but shared with a negative comment could be damaging to your reputation. You can control more than you realize, but only if you are paying attention and talking to the people in your life about how important it is that you maintain a squeaky-clean reputation.

How can you leverage social media?

You make a lot of sacrifices when you commit to a sport, but you don't have to give up everything! We know social media is a great way to stay connected to friends and family and have fun. It's also a way to let everyone know how committed you are to baseball.

Be active and visible

Recruiters and coaches are interested in getting to know the whole player, so it's beneficial to share what genuinely interests you on your social media accounts. Are you interested in chemistry? Share a cool experiment you did in class. Are you a fan of a local sports team? Post a picture of you wearing a team jersey. Share your personality and let them get to know you.

Show the committed side of yourself

As an athlete, you do a lot to stay at the top of your game. Early morning practices, crushing goals, and supporting your teammates are all things you probably do out of habit.

Why not share them on social? There are a lot of fun ways to share how hard you're working. And, as a bonus, your friends and followers can join your journey and cheer you on.

Become a fan

It's easy to get too focused on the content you're putting out into the world and then forget to engage with others! If some colleges and teams interest you, follow them! Engage with their posts and use their social media posts to stay in the loop about college teams and other events.

Follow hashtags

Some platforms use hashtags to connect people interested in a topic. Finding the right hashtag can help you stay up-to-date on important information related to baseball or just what's happening at the school you're interested in. You may find yourself following a few different schools, so hashtags make it much easier to identify relevant topics.

Leverage video

Whether you're active on a video platform like YouTube or a platform that supports video like Facebook or Instagram, post video of yourself practicing or playing. You may enlist the help of your coaches or teammates and encourage them to post on their accounts as well, or you may focus on capturing video yourself. Either way, with cameras in every phone, getting high-quality footage is an easily available option.

If this feels overwhelming, just stop and take a breath! Like we said at the beginning of the chapter, we don't want athletes to be afraid. We also don't want them to think they have to add "maintaining an active social media presence" to their already full schedule! We just want everyone to be aware of the risks and opportunities associated with social media.

To get started, we encourage you to put yourself in the shoes of a coach or recruiter. If someone wants to learn about you – who you are, what you've accomplished, how you approach situations – what will they find online? You can use the following chart to keep track of what you uncover.

1. Begin with a simple internet search (i.e., Google) of the athlete's name and see what comes up.
2. For each social media platform where the athlete has an account, review your last 10 posts or tags.
3. For the platforms where the athlete isn't active, search for the athlete's name or nickname, and review accounts where they may have been mentioned.
4. If any negative posts are found, ask if there is a way the post can be removed.
5. If positive posts are found, consider opportunities that may exist for you to create similar posts in the future.

SOCIAL MEDIA
ASSESSMENT CHART

SOCIAL MEDIA PLATFORM	WHO POSTED (ME, MY FRIEND, MY SCHOOL, ETC.)	POSITIVE, NEGATIVE, OR NEUTRAL?	IF IT'S NEGATIVE, IS THERE A WAY TO HAVE IT REMOVED? IF IT'S POSITIVE, CAN I DO IT AGAIN?

No matter what you uncover, it's always better to know what recruiters and coaches could see. Best case scenario, you may be able to ask people to remove content that could be harmful to your reputation. Worst case scenario, if the content isn't removed, you can learn from the mistake and avoid similar situations in the future.

And, like what we've talked about in other chapters, the best way for a student-athlete to avoid being associated with damaging posts online is for them to stay out of high-risk situations.

Peer Affirmation

We also want to share the concept of peer affirmation with you. It's an important concept to understand and – even if you don't use the term – we're pretty sure you'll be able to relate to the concept.

Peer affirmation refers to the natural tendency we all have to seek the opinion of our friends about various aspects of our lives. When we're thinking about buying something, we may ask for opinions. As we get ready to go see a movie, we ask around about what people have seen. We care about what people in our lives think.

In a lot of cases, peer affirmation is helpful. But with the easy access to feedback from people – oftentimes people we don't even know – online, we may not get the best advice. We encourage athletes to think twice about posting questions online for anyone to answer. And think three times about taking advice about your baseball career from anyone but your coaches and the recruitment professionals you're working with!

What's next?

You've had an opportunity to look at an athlete's digital presence the same way a recruiter would. Now you have the opportunity to think about what you read at the beginning of this chapter and how you can leverage your social media presence.

1. What social media platforms are you/the athlete active on?

2. What additional platforms are the athlete's friends active on (where he may be shown in a photograph or tagged)?

3. Considering the answers to questions 1 & 2, what risks need to be addressed? Think about people who may post controversial content, affiliations with groups that could be damaging to your reputation, or events that could be interpreted negatively.

4. Considering the answer to questions 1 & 2, what opportunities can you capitalize on? List at least three things you could share regularly on social media that accurately demonstrate your commitment to being a successful athlete.

CHAPTER 8

Building Relationships

We spent the last chapter focused on making first impressions and tracking your performance so that when you're ready to meet recruiters and coaches, you start on the right foot. In such a competitive sport, you aren't likely to get a second chance to make a first impression, and that's why we devoted a full chapter to the topic. But it's also important to remember that your first impression is just the beginning. Everything that you're doing is building a relationship.

In the next few chapters, we'll talk about researching schools and managing your reputation. But before we dig too far into those details, we wanted to be clear about why all of this is so important. And we're going to share an example of how one of our star athletes made a great first impression, but perhaps more importantly, set the stage for a successful relationship with a coach.

First, we'd like to tell you a little bit about the young man who made so many good choices and ended up in a program that met all of his expectations. To protect his privacy, we'll call him Joe.

Joe was a first-generation high school athlete. His parents were supportive, but they didn't necessarily know exactly what to expect as Joe's obvious talent emerged and the potential for college scholarships became clear. Even when you can see how much talent you're working with, the competition can still be intimidating. His parents knew from the start they'd need help, so they reached out to us. But more important than that, Joe knew the stats he was seeing in high school wouldn't be relevant in his pursuit of a college scholarship.

The family didn't have a lot of money, but what they didn't have in funds, they made up for in commitment. We gave Joe some feedback about what to wear – khakis and a nice shirt. We asked him what he had learned about the school and he demonstrated to us that he had done his research. But when he went on his college tour, he did something that surprised us all.

As planned, the coach met with the family, but early on, Joe stepped up and demonstrated not only his commitment to baseball but his potential to be more than just an average player. He asked the coach about the team, sharing questions based on the research he had done. He asked the coach what his plans for the team were and what he planned to do soon. He was respectful and informed.

Joe left that day with all of the information he needed to make an informed decision about whether or not the school was a good fit for him. That coach left that day thinking he'd just found the next leader for his team.

What They Want to Know About You
We're proud of Joe and happy to report that everything did work out for him. But it wasn't as simple as making a great first impression when a coach saw him play for the first time or even his extraordinary campus visit. It was the relationship that formed over time. Let's look at how every recruiter or coach selects players to join their team.

> **The eyeball test** – we already talked about the first part of the first impression. Coaches and recruiters look at a group of players and you're added to one list or the other.

From there, they decide who they want to learn more about.

Measurements – if you passed the eyeball test, you're worth a little more investigation. But at this point, the recruiter is looking for details. He'll turn to the five most common measures in baseball – arm strength, foot speed, exit velocity/raw power, fielding, and hitting.

The compete tool – maybe one or more of the standard measurements is exactly what they are looking for. But there's something else they need to see, and that's harder to describe. When they're looking at all of the skilled athletes interested in the next level, they're looking for the ones with drive. They need to know that you are all in.

The bigger picture – they'll want to learn more about you, so they may search your name online and on various social media platforms. They may request a phone call. They may even invite you for a campus visit. They're looking for a player that will fit well on their team, and that involves more than just your performance in the game.

When we talk to and watch players, sometimes people are surprised by the questions we ask. Here are a few of our favorites and exactly what they tell us about the player.

What kinds of grades do you get in school? And, whatever those grades are, could they be better if you applied yourself more?

Some people think we ask about grades because we want to make sure the athlete will have the academic ability to be successful in college. That's the smaller piece of what we're asking. The most important piece of that question is the phrase "if you applied yourself more." When we get to know athletes, one of the most important things we try to learn is how hard they'll work without prompting. Remember: We're looking for that sixth tool — the compete tool. We want to see a motivated person.

The last time you struck out, how did you react?

This is better to observe than it is to ask because many players genuinely can't remember with much accuracy how they responded the last time they struck out or made an error. What do we want to see? Grace under fire. A commitment in their eyes to do it better next time. What don't we want to see? An attempt to blame someone else for their mistake. Eye rolling, yelling, or throwing the bat. While most players would guess coaches and recruiters are looking for players who keep their cool, not everyone realizes how important it is to own and learn from your mistakes.

If I were to look at your room right now, would I find that you made your bed?

If their mom made their bed, that doesn't count! We're looking again for personal responsibility. It's rare to find an athlete who's a self-motivated player and lazy contributor to the family. Seeing how someone maintains their own living space can tell us a lot about how they approach life in general.

Would you say you're ready to answer those questions or any other ones we throw at you as we learn about who you are as a person? If you're not sure, now is a good time to consider just how committed you are to competing at the next level.

A committed athlete has to be diligent in maintaining their image as well as their baseball skills. Coaches and recruiters are building a team. Your skill is a big part of what will catch their attention, but your attitude and commitment to the school and your team are what can tip the scales – for or against you.

Would you be interested in playing for the Yankees?
Over the years, the New York Yankees have taken a tremendous amount of criticism for their strict dress code policy. If you aren't familiar with it, this is what it says (in part):

> **The New York Yankees Appearance Policy**
> All players, coaches and male executives are forbidden to display any facial hair other than mustaches (except for religious reasons), and scalp hair may not be grown below the collar.

As laws change, this policy has become more and more difficult to enforce, but you'll find that most of the Yankees comply. Why? Because professional baseball players pick their battles.

Think about everything we've talked about so far. Does anything stand out to you as something you can't comply with? Does researching a campus visit sound tedious and boring? Do you think changing what you post on social media is an unreasonable request? The good news is that anything that you read that you don't want to do is fully in your control – and you *can* choose not to do it. Our goal is to help you understand what's most likely to get you a scholarship. It's up to you whether you want to take our advice or choose the hard way!

What's next?

This section of the book and especially this last chapter was focused on helping you connect in a meaningful way with coaches and recruiters. The task of standing out in a competitive sport is a daunting one, but our goal was to show you just how many areas you can positively influence with your actions.

In each of the previous chapters, you had an opportunity to answer reflection questions and even set goals. Hang onto those answers and then add anything else you learn about yourself and the opportunities you have after thinking about the following questions.

1. Think about 3 times you made a first impression recently. These don't have to be big first impressions – maybe it was just a clerk at a store or a new student in the class. Replay the event in your mind.

    a) How did you come across? Were you confident and respectful? Did you act distracted or rude? Be honest – this is something you're going to learn from.
    b) How did the person you met come across? What was *your* first impression of them? Why did you feel that way? Try to be as specific as possible when you describe both what you thought of them and why.
    c) What can you learn from what you did well, what you could have done better, or what they did?

2. Reflect on 3 recent "failures" and describe how you responded. Like the first impressions, these don't have to be huge events. It can be as simple as striking out, getting

a lower grade on your exam than you had hoped, or being late for practice.

a) What happened?
b) How did you respond?
c) What happened?
d) How did you respond?
e) What happened?
f) How did you respond?

3. Review each of the scenarios you described in question 2. Were you proud of how you reacted? If not, what do you think you should have done differently?

◆ James L. Gamble & David L. Angeron | 86

CHAPTER 9

Maximizing Exposure

A goal all aspiring baseball players share is the desire to catch the attention of a coach. You may have one or multiple specific teams in mind, or you may just want to engage with any coach looking to bring talent like you to their school. Whatever your goal, we can promise you one thing: A coach isn't going to notice you if you don't put effort into maximizing your exposure!

Another common misconception we want to clear up right off the bat is that there is one thing you should do – one thing that will make or break your ability to be discovered by a coach. A successful baseball player does a lot of different things in an organized and committed fashion. All of their hard work eventually comes together to pay off. They rarely can attribute their success to one action.

Because so many of the athletes we talk to are looking for ideas that will help them stand out and be seen by coaches, we wanted to devote an entire chapter to what you can do to get noticed. Depending on how close you are to graduation, some of these opportunities may be more or less relevant, so we encourage you to craft a plan that will support your specific goals while leveraging your unique resources.

Get Video

Earlier in the book, we talked about the fact that you have a team of people who are supporting you as you work toward playing college baseball. Those people can't do your work for you, but there are some things they can do if you provide them with some specific requests. Capturing video of your games and practices is one area they can help.

Identify Your Level
We cover the myth of having to play Div I a few different ways in this book, but we're going to mention it again here. If somewhere along the line someone told you that your goal was to play Div I ball and you don't even remember why anymore, your first task is to let that idea go. Start from scratch and identify realistically what level you should be playing at. Once you know that, you can create a better plan for your development and target the coaches that are most likely to be interested in you.

Play on Summer Teams and Attend Showcases
Attend a showcase or prospect camp at a local college and use the college coach's interest to estimate your ability level. It's the perfect way to meet coaches and it provides you with an excellent opportunity to confirm what level you're playing at.

Visit Colleges
We devoted a chapter in this book to college visits because there are a lot of benefits to athletes venturing out to college campuses and meeting coaches. There are also a lot of guidelines you need to know about! But don't let those scare you off. If you're interested in a school, take the initiative and tour the campus. Just because you visit a campus doesn't mean you have to attend. When you visit schools, you'll be able to identify more and more easily the things that are important to your success as an athlete and as a student.

Hire Help

The earlier you hire a professional to help you choose schools, get noticed by coaches, secure scholarships, and even hit personal goals, the more they'll be able to help you. Make the decision as early as possible and maximize the potential benefits.

Take or Retake Your SAT/ACT

You don't have to be very far into your recruiting process to have learned that grades and test scores matter to coaches. You may have what they need on their team, but if there's an indication you won't cut it as a student, they'll move on to the next player. Have your grades available and your tests completed early.

Register with the NCAA Eligibility Center

This is a process we also mentioned earlier in the book, and the good news is that the steps are very clearly outlined online. The bad news is that there are quite a few steps to follow! But once you've registered, coaches will be able to find you and you will have once again demonstrated a desirable level of professionalism that can help you stand out in the crowd.

When you meet coaches and recruiters, this list of ideas for maximizing your exposure will grow, but a few things will always remain the same.

1. Getting coaches to notice you is up to you. Your family, friends, and high school coaches will help you, but the more active you are in your success, the more likely you are to achieve the results you're looking for.

2. Talent and luck are only part of the equation – the biggest contribution to your success will be consistent hard work. A lot of what we listed include things like taking tests and filling out forms – not the first thing most athletes think of when they imagine a coach inviting them to play on their team! But the majority of the time, it's that kind of work that secures your future.

3. Constructive feedback and even rejection are part of the process. No matter who you are, not every coach will want you on their team. The question becomes whether or not constructive feedback fuels you to do better or convinces you to give up.

The most important thing to remember about increasing your visibility is that there isn't any one thing that will make you successful. Your best chance at being seen will come from you boosting your visibility from as many angles and using as many tools as possible!

What's next?
We're sure you read through this chapter and identified a few different areas where you can do more than you're doing now. Whether it's something small and fun like researching showcases or big and scary like committing to retake your SATs, your next step is to make commitments around what you can do to support your success.

1. Review each of the items discussed in this chapter. Identify three that you can commit to doing.

2. For each of the three items you committed to, answer the following questions.

   a) Why is this important to your success as an athlete?
   b) What obstacles can you anticipate and how will you overcome them?
   c) Who, if anyone, can help you and what resources do you have access to that can help you be successful?

♦ James L. Gamble & David L. Angeron|92

CHAPTER 10

Choosing the right camps, showcases, and teams

Choosing camps and showcases throughout your baseball career is important and it may not be as easy as it sounds. Where should you begin? If you're considering playing college baseball, you probably know the difference between baseball camps and showcases, but just to make sure we're on the same page before getting too far into this chapter, we'll start with some definitions.

Camps are like college baseball practices. Athletes meet and work directly with coaches.

Showcases are designed for players who want to demonstrate their skills in front of college coaches. They typically consist of workout sessions and a minimum of one game.

Seeing the definitions side-by-side, we hope the differences make the benefits of both clear. Showcases serve the important purpose of highlighting your skills and camps are the perfect opportunities to develop specific competencies. With that in mind, we're going to explore tips for both.

Camps

Summer and winter camps are a great place for players to go to develop their skills. They can work directly with talented coaches who will take a personalized approach to provide guidance and feedback for each player. The most common categories developed in camps include:

- Hitting techniques like strike zone discipline, pitch recognition, approach, bunting, and situational hitting
- Pitching techniques like arm care, delivery, mechanics, fielding practice, and off-speed development
- Baserunning, stealing, sliding, reading cues, and primary or secondary leads
- Catching, blocking, throwing, receiving, and game calling

More general topics are also often covered including:

- Infield tactics and skills
- Outfield tactics and skills
- Team fundamentals
- General physical development

Since about 500,000 high school students play baseball each year and less than 2 percent will be recruited, camps are one of several effective ways to get in front of the coaches who may eventually want to add you to their team. But more importantly, attend a camp to develop your skills and gain a competitive edge.

Tips for Choosing the Best Camps

Every camp is not created equal and every player may have different goals and needs that can be supported by a camp. To help you decide the best camps that will develop your skills, answer the following questions:

1. What are my goals for attending a baseball camp?

2. What feedback have my coaches given me that could help me identify areas I can improve?

Once you've answered those questions, you can consider the following points and choose the camp that will best support your development.

Invest time in searching. A lot of people ask us how they should start searching for camps and what they should look for. Luckily, the internet makes this kind of information gathering easy – when you know what questions to ask. Search for baseball camps in your area and then, at their websites, look at the program design. As we'll advise later in this section, you want to make sure the right skill areas are being covered, but you also want to identify the ratio of coaches to players to make sure you'll receive the amount of attention you want.

Choose the right camp for your age and skill level. Don't sign up for a camp just because someone you know is attending or because you received an email inviting you to attend. Do your research and identify the age and skill level the camp supports to ensure you get the most out of your investment of time and money.

Find the camp that will focus on the skills you want to develop. One camp may be more convenient, or it may have a broader offering that looks appealing but remember why you're there. If there's a camp that focuses on a skill you want to develop, they're more likely to have the best staff to provide you with valuable feedback.

Be realistic about costs. The costs of camps range from $100 to thousands of dollars depending on duration and what's offered. Know what your family budget is, explore scholarship options, and then show up and do your best work at the camp that makes the most financial sense.

Showcases

Your goal when you attend a showcase is to stand out. You have an opportunity to stand out at a camp as well, but a camp also has the goal of player development. When you're at a showcase, you're there to be seen.

With that in mind, here are a few tips to remember.

- Don't go if you're sick or injured. Coaches are making snap decisions and aren't going to wait around to ask how you're feeling. If you're underperforming, they'll assume that's your best possible performance and you'll have made an unnecessarily bad first impression.
- Know what to expect at the showcase. Do your research and as much as possible show up knowing exactly what you'll be asked to do. This will allow you to practice the exact formula in advance, and that will boost your confidence and performance.
- Remember that at any point in time a coach could be evaluating you — not just when you think you're being assessed. Look professional and engaged during the entire showcase.

Tips for choosing the best showcases
There are a lot of showcases available and it may feel overwhelming when you start to look at them all! There's no reason to feel overwhelmed, though. Just follow a few simple steps and you'll get to where you need to be.

- Leverage the resources you have available. Ask your coaches or anyone else familiar with the process and your goals for their advice and recommendations.
- Find as many details as you possibly can online. Look at who will be at the showcase, where it will be located, and what the design is. This way you can make the most informed decision before investing any time or money.

Important things to remember as you prepare for a camp or showcase

- Pay attention to your schedule! Before attending, don't overexert yourself. If you're rundown or sore, you'll be sluggish. The coaches observing you will assume that what they are seeing is your best game and may write your off before getting to know any more about you.
- Show up early. There's no reason to increase your anxiety by cutting your schedule close. Pad your schedule so that you can manage anything unexpected.

Important things to remember once you arrive

- Once you arrive at a camp or showcase, assume you're always being observed. This means you show up to scheduled events early, speak respectfully to those around you – players, coaches, support staff, and dress in clean, presentable clothes.
- Be aware of your body language. Stand up straight and look confident – even if you don't feel 100% confident! You'll be amazed by how much looking confident will help you feel confident.
- During warm-up periods or downtime, do what you need to do to take care of yourself. If you need to do additional stretching or jog in place to stay warm, pay attention to your body. You're responsible for your performance, so don't look to others for cues about what you should be doing.
- Remember to breathe. It's normal to be nervous and you can prepare for those feelings! If you arrive and are hit by a wave of nerves, just take a few deep breaths. You can calm yourself down in less than a minute with this simple technique! And then before you know it, you'll be talking to people and playing the game you love, and you'll be too busy to be nervous.
- Don't under any circumstances lean against a wall or fence – it makes you look lazy and uninterested. Remember that at any point in time you may be making a first impression on a coach. It may not seem fair, but that's the way it happens! You have to continually be on your best behavior.

Tips for making an impression with your skills
Coaches are looking for a variety of things when they show up at camps and showcases, so don't' focus on what you think they want to see. Focus on what you know are your strengths. Whatever category sets you apart, here are some ideas for really standing out.

Foot speed

- You'll probably be running a 60-yard dash, so practice a 60-yard dash. Like practicing an obstacle course or throwing repeatedly, repetition will help you feel more comfortable and confident, and in the end, you'll perform better.
- Stay warm – especially if you're at the end of a line. Jog in place and keep your muscles ready to run. As a bonus, this kind of activity will also help keep you mentally engaged and give coaches the clear impression that you are a serious player.
- Give your best to the end and then some. Don't slow down as you approach the finish line. Push past the finish line and slow down once you know you've crossed.

Defense

- It may look a little different, but apply the same rule we recommended for the 60-yard dash: Stay warm. Play catch inline or stretch while you wait.
- Coaches are typically looking for strength over accuracy at these events. Accuracy is still important, it's just second to

power. Don't psych yourself out striving for perfection. Give every throw all you've got.

- If you can, gather information about what the exercises will look like and then practice those exact skill demonstrations. Like the benefit of practicing the exact running distance you'll be assessed on, you can build confidence by practicing some or all of the specific plays that will be executed.
- Always make an effort. If you need to dive to make a catch, then dive to make the catch! Can't get to the ball fast enough to stop it? Run it out anyway. Coaches notice skill, of course, but they know the ball doesn't always bounce your way. They'll notice the effort and your attitude toward the game, too.

Offense

- Your round of hitting has the potential to be incredibly stressful, so prepare yourself mentally. This is always a good recommendation, but with hitting especially, it can be easy for athletes to succumb to the pressure. The best way to combat those feelings is to be prepared for them!
- Stay warm! Are you noticing a pattern here? Like running and defensive work, it's up to you to take care of yourself! If there's a warm-up station, use it. If not, find other ways to keep your muscles warm.
- Don't be afraid to take a pitch if you need it to assess the pitcher. If you can, learn as much as possible before you get to the plate. But once you're there, if you need a pitch to get a feel for timing, take it. Consider it an investment in the rest of your hits.

Pitching

- Coaches are primarily looking at your velocity, location, and changing speeds. You know this going in, so you know what to work on in advance!
- Show command of your pitches by throwing low strikes and off-speed pitches.
- At the end of your time, you can use a few pitches to let loose and show them what you've got!

What's next?

Now that you've had a chance to think a little more about the goal of camps and showcases, we'd like you to make some important decisions and put them in writing.

1. Identify your goals for attending camps and showcases. For example, you may have a goal of attending a camp to improve a specific skill or a showcase at a specific time to secure early interest with a coach.

2. Create a timeline. Starting with where you are when you're reading this book, create a timeline that includes the following:
    a) From question 1, note what goals you'd like to accomplish by when. For example, based on industry averages, you may be aiming for multiple specific 60-yard dash times as you mature and gain experience. Include those on your timeline.

  b) Note all of the possible camps and showcases you're interested in, including their dates, locations, and costs.

With these details, you'll have a picture of your goals and options. You can update it over time, marking things you've completed, adding events, or removing options that are no longer of interest.

3. Research camps and showcases that support your goals and meet your timeline. When completing your research, remember to look up exactly how the camp is run so you understand what kind of coaching and feedback you'll be receiving.

CHAPTER 11

Myths

We hope that as a result of reading this book, you feel informed and empowered to be recruited by the college of your dreams! We also hope that we've been able to correct any incorrect information you've heard over the years. There is a lot to keep track of and even the most informed players sometimes get bad information!

There are a few baseball recruiting myths we want to make sure to dispel — and some of them have come up more than once already, but they bear repeating! Knowledge is power, so we want you to compete with all the right information.

Recruiting begins your senior year.
We understand where this misunderstanding comes from. From the outside, it *looks* like recruiting begins in an athlete's senior year of high school because that's when there's typically a significant increase in activity. But if you wait to *start* the process until then, you will undoubtedly find yourself wanting to accomplish goals that require more time than you have. Nothing's impossible, but it is harder to get to where you need to be when you start the recruiting process late.

There's only one way to get drafted.
While a lot of players are drafted from Div I schools, plenty come from other divisions. The players that are drafted are the ones that are in the environment that allows them to play their best and showcase their talent. A lot of talented players end up at Division

I schools, but a lot don't because they realize their best-fit is at a different school.

Division III Schools are weaker athletically.
There are Division III programs that are weaker than Div I and Div II schools, but there are also many that have talented athletic programs. MLB scouts find their talent in all three divisions, so finding the school that's the best fit for you and allows you to showcase your talent is your best plan.

If I can't get into the school I want, I can just play for a Div III school.
We love confidence, but don't think just anyone can play for a Div III school or play as a walk-on at your first-choice university. If you think you can just stroll onto a Div III program you are in for a surprise. If you haven't watched a top 25 Div III game and you think this way you are severely limiting your choices.

If you're good enough, college coaches will find you.
Whether it's because of the rare and admittedly entertaining success stories of how athletes are discovered in unusual ways or just because we all like the idea that there's a chance we won't have to do much work, this is a myth people love to believe! The truth is, it's rare for an athlete to be discovered after no work on their part. College coaches are busy, and they receive a lot of communications and recommendations, so they use their time wisely. It's possible they could come out to meet someone else and end up seeing you, but it isn't likely. And besides, you want to be responsible for your discovery and success, don't you?

There's one (or maybe two) tournaments and/or showcases every serious athlete must attend.
There are certainly some tournaments and showcases that are frequently and highly recommended, but there isn't a single make-or-break event any athlete has to attend.

If you want to play MLB, you have to play on one of a few specific college teams.
Like the camps and showcases, there isn't any *one* team that's required for an athlete interested in playing MLB. It is far more important that the big picture the school can offer you fits your developmental goals – the right coach, an opportunity to play, and an academic program that's a fit for you.

Once you commit to a school, that's where you have to go.
We talk about visiting schools, talking to coaches, and receiving a letter of intent in other chapters, but we wanted to emphasize here that verbally committing to a school doesn't mean you're required to attend – just like a coach expressing interest in you doesn't mean they'll extend a scholarship offer. A lot of what happens between players and coaches in the years that their skills are developing is just conversations. You'll change and their needs will change and you may end up a perfect match. You may also find a different school that's a better fit for you.

Coaches don't like being contacted by athletes.
Why wouldn't a coach want to hear from a committed athlete who is responsible enough to take ownership of their professional success? We get it – no one wants to be perceived as a pest and rule themselves out of scholarship opportunities right off the bat because all a coach can remember about them is that they are

annoying. But if you follow the guidelines we've offered in this book in your conversations, you'll be perceived as a young professional.

All colleges offer athletic scholarships
Remember that your success playing college ball has many components – including the financial commitment. Even if you are their top choice and exactly what a team needs, not all colleges can offer scholarships. Division I and Division II colleges, junior colleges, and some NAIA schools can offer athletic scholarships. Division III colleges can only offer financial aid and academic grants.

Real, committed athletes get a full scholarship
Because most teams have a pool of scholarship money. full scholarships are rare. Coaches are more likely to divide scholarship money up between multiple critical players. If you find yourself in that pool and are offered a partial scholarship, it is an accomplishment to be proud of!

Baseball lasts forever.
Those of us that love baseball would like to think that it lasts forever, but we all know it doesn't. But if it's something we all know, why bother busting the myth? We talk to all of our players about setting themselves up for a successful future, with or without a professional baseball career. You may have an amazing college career, get drafted and play major league baseball for years, thereby securing a healthy financial future. You may have an amazing college career and pursue a career as a marketer as soon as you graduate. You may land somewhere in the middle – play in the majors for two years and then pursue a different career. Whatever

path you take, we just want to help you keep as many options open for as long as possible. Whether you're experiencing highs or lows, just remember to keep your options open.

What's next?
We covered a lot of different topics in this chapter, so you may be wondering how we're going to bring it all together! It's simple – we're going to ask you to be honest with yourself about any misconceptions you had and even identify questions you're still wondering about!

1. Take a look at the list of myths we busted in this chapter. Which ones were new information to you? And what related myths do you think you need to resolve? For example, if you hadn't ever really thought about what schools offered scholarships, you may choose to invest time in researching all of the scholarship guidelines to see what else you may not be aware of.
2. Make a list of any other questions you may have. Sometimes reading a long list of answers can leave a person with a long list of questions! Take the initiative to get the correct information by taking your questions to your coach, guidance counselor, etc. so you can be confident you're continually working with the facts that will help you accomplish your goal.

CHAPTER 12

Cost of Getting Recruited

There are a lot of fantastic stories that we hear about successful baseball players that seem to have a magical recruitment experience. The way the story is told makes their journey sound effortless, even if part of the story focuses on overcoming obstacles. But in the real world, securing a college scholarship requires a significant investment from the athlete and their family. And that investment includes money as well as time!

Creating a financial plan
Depending on where you're at in your baseball career, some or all of the following tips may be useful. Remember to apply what's relevant to your path and make a note of any additional considerations that may be unique to your journey!

Gear
Considering the bigger investments we'll talk about later in this chapter, it may seem trivial, but players do need gear and you should calculate the purchase and maintenance of that gear into your costs. The basics include a bat, ball, baseball and batting gloves, cleats, and protective gear. Different positions may require additional gear (like catchers), so consider that as well!

Teams

The possible costs of joining a team have such a wide range, it's difficult to estimate what any individual athlete will end up investing. However, it is easy enough to inquire about basic fees. After that, we do encourage you to think about the additional costs that may not be apparent when you're joining a team. For example, you may join a traveling team for $800. An important question to ask is whether that fee includes hotel costs and tournament fees. It may not change your mind about joining or choosing another league, but at the very least you'll avoid being surprised by expenses you hadn't considered.

Athlete Advancement Professional

We meet athletes at different points in their journey. Some recognize early on that to compete for scholarships, they need professional support. Others come to the sport or recognize the level of their talent later and reach a similar conclusion – with a shorter window to make an impact, they need an expert in their corner. When you explore investing in a relationship with an athlete advancement professional, there are typically a variety of ways to engage support with varying costs associated with the level of support requested. When inquiring, keep in mind what your unique strengths and needs are and invest accordingly.

Camps & Showcases

Similar to teams, camps and showcases also vary in cost and also may have additional costs associated with them that you need to remember. As always, keep your goal in mind and balance that with the options you have. If you're looking to improve your hitting, there are likely several camps that will be helpful for you. If the price is a concern or if your money could be better spent elsewhere, the variety of choices you have may be a great opportunity to save some of your funds.

Academic Tutoring

In some cases, excellent tutors may be available for students free of charge, but you'll probably need to budget to pay a tutor on an hourly basis. Rate averages can be found with a quick internet search and will be accurate enough for creating a general budget for tutoring expenses.

Creating a Schedule

At the start of this chapter, we mentioned that there's an investment of money *and time* that's required for anyone following a recruitment plan. Now that you have a bit of an understanding of the financial component, let's look at the time you and your family will need to invest.

Showing Up Early and Staying Late

If you're committed enough to baseball to secure an athletic scholarship, we won't have to encourage you to show up early for practice, stay late as needed, and refine your skills between practices at home. You'll naturally do that out of your love for the game! However, we wanted to list those considerations here because those commitments require time that needs to be accounted for in your schedule and oftentimes your family members are affected, too. Getting rides to practices and games, extra trips for additional practice, and a flexible household chore schedule that allows you to be a contributing member in your household while still balancing an active training schedule all require a lot of communication with your family members, coaches, and teammates.

We recommend partnering with other families for carpooling and sharing expenses whenever possible! Not only does it cut the time commitment down in a lot of instances, but it can also often decrease each family's financial commitment! And everything is more fun with friends, so working with a teammate to get in extra practice time is just more enjoyable!

Teams, Camps, and Showcases
Athletes and their families tend to focus on the total financial commitment associated with joining teams, camps, and showcases, but there's an important time commitment to remember, too. Travel time, the length of the event, and any preparation needed should be factored in, especially if there are conflicting obligations. For example, if a camp is offered at the same time an important school event is being held, you may have to decide which one you'll attend.

Recruitment Video
Recruitment videos have come up a few times, so we'll just quickly remind you that it requires some planning to create a recruitment video and time to edit and share the finished product. Each athlete has their own unique set of skills in this area, so it's hard to estimate exactly what you will need. However, we do encourage you to allow yourself time to capture video – you may need several practices and games to get the footage you want – as well as time to edit and then share the finished product.

Academic Tutoring

By now we hope we've convinced you that coaches are looking for a well-rounded student who plays hard on the field and is an equally committed academic. The simplest way to demonstrate your commitment to your classes is by getting good grades but earning those grades may not be easy. That's where your commitment to baseball translates to meeting with tutors as needed to keep your grades where they need to be.

Putting it all together

This is an incredibly important decision you and your family need to make together! What kind of time and money can you commit to your baseball career? And, maybe most importantly, what will have to give up?

- Are you willing to give up hanging out with friends after school so that you can put the extra time into studying and refining your baseball skills?
- Do your parents, older siblings, or family friends have flexible enough work schedules that they can take you to and from practices as needed?
- Can your guidance counselor recommend a tutor to help you with coursework as needed?
- Can you attend the baseball camps you're interested in? If not, are there alternative programs that are equally appealing?

When we meet with parents who talk about having to motivate their kids to get to practice and do their homework, we usually tell them their young athlete simply doesn't have the drive it takes to secure a college scholarship playing baseball. We're not saying it's ever easy, but a passion for the game will be what motivates you to keep trying when you can't seem to hit your 60-yard dash goal. A passion for the game is what will help you meet with a math tutor when all you want to do is head home and relax. It's your passion for the game that will help you find your unique path to finding the time and money to succeed in a baseball career.

What's next?
We've given you a lot to think about related to your finances, your time, and your level of commitment. Now it's time to answer some of these questions in writing. You were probably answering a lot of them in your head as you read the chapter, but you'll find that writing out your answer will take your understanding up a notch.

1. Of the financial commitments listed in this chapter, which ones do you need to research and verify for yourself? In other words, what potential costs had you not yet considered or are still unclear?
2. What alternatives, if any are needed, do you have available to you?
3. What time commitments will be challenging for you and your family?

CHAPTER 13

DI or Bust

We already talked about the myth that baseball players have to play on a Div I team and we hope you got the message that there isn't any single path to success for a committed player. The most important thing you can do is look at the big picture and ask yourself where you'll get to play and what college will help you accomplish your goals?

Even though we share this advice repeatedly, we're not always sure it sticks. To make our point, we wanted to use this chapter to highlight a few players you've probably heard of whose path to success didn't include time at a Div I school.

JD Martinez
In 2009, Martinez was picked up by the Houston Astros in the amateur draft. He attended Nova Southeastern University, a Div II school in Florida. He's since played for the Detroit Tigers, Boston Red Sox, and the Houston Astros. In his career so far, a few of his accomplishments include:

- Two-time selection for the MLB All-Star Game
- Three-time Silver Slugger Award winner

Martinez is also forever in the record books for being the 18th person in MLB history to hit four home runs in a single game.

Ben Zobrist

Zobrist (also known as Zorilla) attended Olivet Nazarene University, an NAIA institution. He played second base and was an outfielder for several MLB teams. What's he known for?

- Played in three World Series…and won two of them
- Versatility – he's a switch-hitter and has played second base, shortstop, and outfield

Zobrist is one of only seven players in the history of major league baseball to have won back-to-back World Series championships on different teams.

Albert Pujols

Pujols played for a junior college before he was drafted by the Cardinals. He's enjoyed a long career playing first base. In that time, he experienced some impressive highs including:

- a unanimous vote for Rookie of the Year
- three National League MVP awards
- nine All-Star game appearances
- two World Series championships

Like a lot of successful baseball players, Pujols worked hard and brought a wide range of skills to the teams he played for.

What can you learn from each of these players? We'll all have a different takeaway, but we hope one thing you can't miss is how different their paths were. They saw the opportunities that were right for them and pursued them. They worked hard. They didn't give up and they were rewarded for their commitment.

What happens after college?

Another important reason we don't want you to discount schools that aren't Div I is that the overwhelming majority of successful college baseball players don't go on to play professionally. We shared the stories of successful college baseball players who went on to play in the majors, but what about everyone else?

Other successful college players graduate and have a job working in a field they love. If that's your path, it may be a Div II or Div III school that allows you to study what you're passionate about. The big picture is more important than the most popular path!

What's Next?
Now's a good time to take a moment to widen your search. Are there any schools you ruled out because they weren't Div I? Are there things you want to study that you didn't find at your top schools? Maybe not! You may end up with the same list of schools you started with, but we hope you'll expand your search just to be sure!

1. Do some research on the schools you're interested in! Have any of their players registered records while playing college baseball or gone on to play professionally?

2. Expand your school list! Especially if you had restricted your list to only Div I schools, add a few Div II and Div III schools to the mix if they fit your criteria.

CHAPTER 14

Committing: Early vs Late

It is understandable when a young athlete – freshman or sophomore in high school – is committed. We completely get why the student-athlete feels amazing and tells all of their friends that they already know what college they're going to. We also understand why parents are so eager to commit early and have one less thing to worry about.

Committing vs. signing

We wanted to start this chapter by talking about the difference between committing and signing. Some people will use the terms interchangeably, but they don't mean the same thing.

When you commit to a school, it means you've expressed an interest in them and they've expressed an interest in you. It's something to be proud of and excited about!

When you sign with a school, you complete a letter of intent. It's only when you sign that you and the school are bound to your agreement. We talk about signing a letter of intent in another chapter, but because we hear the misuse so often, we wanted to clarify the language early in this chapter!

There are a lot of risks associated with committing early and a lot of misinformation about the process as well. In this chapter – even though we don't want to take anything away from the excitement of early interest from a college or university – our goal is to help athletes and their families understand what committing early really means.

Why is it so tempting to commit early?
When we talk to athletes and their families about committing early, part of what we hear is the pride and excitement that comes naturally with the opportunity. But another big motivator – especially for the parents – is relief. It can feel good to see security in your kid's future! The earlier that safety arrives the better.

The problem with that feeling of relief is that it isn't accurate. Parents should feel proud and we hope they enjoy how happy an early offer has made the young athlete in their family feel. But if they think their hard work has paid off and they can coast through the next few years, they are wrong – and that misinformation could be costly.

What does committing early *really* mean?
When a young athlete commits early and doesn't sign a letter of intent, all the athlete and school are agreeing on is that there is a mutual interest between the two. At any time, the athlete can change their mind and the coach can de-commit the athlete.

Why would coaches bother to reach out to athletes so early if the offer wasn't official? It isn't that the coaches aren't genuine in their interest. Odds are, at the time of the offer, they genuinely believe there will be a place on the team for the athlete. They are looking that far into the future. Like a chess game, the way you win is to be thinking five moves ahead of where you are now. The difference with recruiting players is that these coaches don't know how that athlete is going to change over the years and what other talented players may emerge.

What are the risks?
Athletes and parents often wonder if committing early is risky because it eliminates future opportunities. What if the athlete

becomes interested in another school? What if another school becomes interested in them? As we already shared, committing early isn't an enforceable agreement, so those concerns aren't anything to be worried about. There are risks associated with committing early, though.

The younger you are, the more you'll change before college.

As we already mentioned, even though coaches are experts at spotting talent, they can't predict the future. You may change physically before you're ready to play on a college team, and the earlier you commit, the more time there is for those changes to occur. Your interests may change, too. At the end of your freshman year, you may become interested in studying at a different college or even end up playing a different position on your high school team. You or the coach may change your mind because of these changes that could naturally happen.

The college may change their mind – and that can be a crushing blow to an athlete's spirit.

For whatever reason, if a coach decides to de-commit – and remember that they can do so at any time because committing early isn't a binding contract – that's a hard thing for any athlete to hear. Even if the athlete was starting to lose interest or the coach has a perfectly understandable reason, it's still a painful rejection. And if the athlete blasted their early commitment all over social media and have been wearing the university's gear for a few years, now they have to explain to everyone why their plans have changed. It's an unnecessary risk that can be devastating to a young athlete's success. The fact is, there may be a change in what the team needs or you may suffer an injury – nothing you should feel badly about. But it still hurts and it can be avoided.

The athlete may feel pressured to honor their early commitment, even though their needs and interests have changed.

We've talked a lot about the fact that a coach may change their mind, but the athlete may change their mind, too. At fourteen, not many people know what they want to study in college or do for a career. In high school, you're likely to discover new potential areas of interest that you may want to study and the school you committed may not offer what you need. Understanding that committing early doesn't mean you have to go to that college is important, but again, you can avoid the awkward conversation of telling the coach you've changed your mind if you simply don't commit too early.

Once committed, an athlete may lose their motivation to improve.

We talk a lot about motivation in this book and it's important to remember that everyone is motivated in different ways and to different degrees. The concerning trend that we've seen has been when a young athlete is committed early, they take their foot off the gas. They don't play as hard. Their grades slip. Because they don't feel like they need to impress anyone anymore, they aren't working as hard as they used to. Sometimes the change is subtle, and sometimes the change is dramatic. But whatever the negative impact, it is again an unnecessary complication.

You may have noticed a theme in this list. The majority of potential issues associated with committing early are related to motivation and performing at your best. You may think you aren't at risk because of how motivated you are now! We can tell you that everyone is at risk. We can also tell you there's no reason to make your life more difficult than it has to be. Managing your motivation is just as important as any other part of your preparation for college.

Have you considered the benefits of being overlooked?
Everyone wants to be acknowledged and appreciated. But have you ever thought about how motivating it is to have someone not express an interest in you? If you're reading this chapter and wondering why no one has tried to sign you early, consider the bright side. When we find young athletes who have that compete tool – that unstoppable drive – and they haven't yet been discovered, it only fuels their fire. They work harder. They do more. Their focus intensifies.

This is a long journey. Those who peak early may find themselves at a disadvantage because few things are more motivating than someone telling you that you can't do something.

Maintaining Psychological Momentum
It's a big request, but we want to encourage you to think twice about committing early. Relieving your anxiety about the future is tempting but remember that it's not real relief. You or the coach may change your mind and committing won't stop either of you.

The risk to your momentum is real, though. If you feel like you've arrived, you may make different choices. We're talking about small choices – skipping a practice, not studying for a test, or ignoring your current coach's advice. Bad choices add up and slow you down. When you stop, someone is going to catch you.

What's Next?
A hard conversation we have to have with a lot of athletes and their families is about mindset. Working for years toward a goal is hard work and stressful. There are so many opportunities to take an easy way or to do less than your best. Now is the time to identify areas where you may be at risk and the things you can do to stay motivated!

1. Assess your motivation – ask yourself some hard questions!
   a) Do you have to be encouraged to go to practice?
   b) Are you getting the best grades you could earn in all of your classes?
2. Talk to a college athlete in your community. Ask them about their experience, what they'd do differently, and what they're glad they did!

CHAPTER 15

Financial Aid

Part of figuring out where you're going to go to college is figuring out how you're going to pay for college. It's fun to talk about your talent, what you've accomplished, and the pros and cons of each of the schools you're interested in. But it's critical to talk about how the financial commitment associated with continuing your education will affect your family and your future.

There are multiple common ways people pay for college, and most people use a combination of approaches.

- **Athletic Scholarships** – We help student-athletes identify opportunities for full or partial scholarships based on their ability to contribute to the school's athletic team. These scholarships are competitive, and schools look at more than just your ability to play baseball. Your performance as a student and community service are also often considered.
- **Academic Scholarships** – Like athletic scholarships, academic scholarships are competitive and often look at the whole student, not just their grades. But if you commit early to pursuing an athletic scholarship by studying more and earning good grades, you may find there are academic scholarships with your name on them, too.
- **Private Scholarships** – Ask your guidance counselor or do a quick search online for private scholarships you may be eligible for. You may find that someone in your community is offering scholarships to people who graduate from your high school or someone else offering

a scholarship based on financial need. You never know unless you inquire and, if you're eligible, apply!

- **Grants** – When you apply for financial aid – and you should always at least apply for financial aid – you may find that you are eligible for a grant from the college, the state, or the federal government. In most cases, grants are awarded based on financial need, but you never know what you will qualify for, and it doesn't hurt to apply. An important piece to remember when budgeting is that grants are different from loans because grants don't have to be paid back.
- **Student Loans** – You'll also see what student loans you are eligible for when you apply for financial aid. These do require repayment, but not until after you graduate.
- **Private Payment** – If you and your family save for your college, you may have the opportunity to make private payments to the university as your tuition is due.

> No matter what, it's likely you'll need to use multiple forms of payment to cover your college expenses. Scholarships alone won't cover all of your costs. Consider all of your options so you can make an informed decision when you need to.

With so many different options, it's important to take the time to identify what payment – or more likely, what payments – will work best. It's also important to remember that your approach may change from year to year. For example, maybe you have a partial athletic scholarship and can make a private payment in your first year and then switch to student loans for your second year. **How much money do you need for college anyway?**

For most college students, their freshman year in college is their first time living away from home. Even the smartest students can be surprised by how many expenses there are associated that come with being out on your own! Everyone will have a slightly different list and every item on that list will be different for each person, but here are some considerations to get you started.

- **Tuition**

    Your tuition costs will be pretty easy for you to estimate! Be sure to include any additional fees you can anticipate. The universities you're interested in can provide you with all of the details you need.

- **Room and Board**

    Have you decided where you're going to live? Unless you're staying at home (assuming your parents aren't charging you rent), you'll need to cover the costs of on or off-campus housing. Sharing housing is a good way to curb expenses, but we recommend you find someone who shares your commitment to sports and doing well in school. Surrounding yourself with like-minded people can help you stay focused.

- **Books and Other School Supplies**

    The cost of textbooks can add up and, depending on what you're studying, you may have lab fees or other resources you'll need to purchase. Oftentimes you can get an estimate of what you should expect to spend, but if not, it's a good idea to set some money aside just in case.

- **Transportation**

    Depending on what city you're in and whether or not you'll need to travel much, you'll need to decide if you need a vehicle, bus pass, or access to some other mode of transportation. If you do keep a car on campus, make sure to research all associated expenses like parking and insurance costs.

- **Food and Clothing**
  One shocking realization many college freshmen have is that their parents have been spending a lot of money to feed and clothe them all these years! You may choose a meal plan through the university or to buy groceries on your own, but no matter what, you'll need a budget to cover those expenses.

- **Fun Money**
  You will be busy with baseball and school, but you'll still have a chance to catch a movie and go out to dinner occasionally. It's important to have that money set aside and give yourself breaks when you need them.

Research each of these categories and determine what you'll need to cover all of your bases. The earlier you start saving, the easier it will be to find a funding approach that works!

Ask the Colleges How They Can Help

If you've made some connections on campus, you may already have an inside track to financial support through the college. Inquire with your coach, student services, or any other resources on campus about student housing resources, on-campus jobs, discounted shopping for students, etc. You'll be amazed at what tricks you'll learn and how quickly the savings will add up if you ask around for help.

A Financial Path That Makes Sense for Your Family

You've heard us mention this already, but we wanted to address it one more time because it is important. For many families, paying for your college is a family decision. Whether they provide partial or full support if they are part of the decision. Organizing all of the information you'll need by following the guidelines in this chapter will help you make thorough and informed decisions.

What's next?

I think you can probably guess that our advice for the end of this chapter is for you to create a budget! Remember to complete the following steps for all of the schools you're interested in. Depending on tuition, cost of living, and a variety of other factors, you may find the costs associated with different schools vary more than you realize!

1. Talk to your family about the financial resources you'd like to explore. Research what's involved in applying for financial aid and any scholarships that may be available.
2. Complete an estimated budget. When needed, ask for the detailed numbers you need to accurately complete the form. The closer your estimates are, the better!

CHAPTER 16

Letter of Intent

Your Letter of Intent is the agreement that matters. A National Letter of Intent (NLI) is a two-way commitment between the player and the school. Earlier in the book, we talked about early committing and verbal agreements, but an NLI is different. It is a binding contract and should be treated very seriously.

A logical place to begin this chapter is by defining what a letter of intent is. We do find that many athletes and their families are a little fuzzy about the exact details of the purpose and value, and that uncertainty can lead to challenges for athletes in any sport.

A letter of intent indicates that you agree to attend an institution for one year in exchange for the institution's written commitment to provide you athletic financial aid for the entire academic year. The benefits – particularly the security that comes with a written commitment – is appealing, but there is another side to the deal.

> *Specifically, by signing an NLI, you agree to attend the institution for one year in exchange for the institution's promise, in writing, to provide you athletics financial aid for the entire academic year. Simply, by signing an NLI you are given an award including athletics aid for the upcoming academic year provided you are admitted to the institution and you are eligible for athletics aid under NCAA rules. Furthermore, by signing an NLI you effectively end the recruiting process. Once you sign an NLI, a recruiting ban goes into effect and you may no longer be recruited by any other NLI school.*
>
> nationalletter.org

The temptation to sign a letter of intent is strong and in many cases, you should sign! But we wanted to devote a chapter in this book specifically to letters of intent because there are so many misunderstandings that emerge when they are offered to athletes. We want you to be fully informed so that when you do have an offer in front of you, you can stay calm and collected, making the best decision for your professional baseball career.

Like a few of the other chapters, we felt the best way to share the most important points with you would be through the questions we hear most often.

Is there a signing date?
Yes, there is a signing date that signifies the first date a player is able to sign a letter of intent. But that date is only the beginning – and it changes every year.

What athletes should sign an NLI?
Student-athletes enrolling in a four-year institution for the first time are eligible to sign an NLI. Student-athletes who start their academic career at a four-year institution and then transfer to a two-year college may also sign an NLI if they plan on entering a second four-year institution.

Does signing guarantee I will play?
Signing an NLI doesn't guarantee you playing time or even a spot on the team. Signing an NLI means the institution agrees to provide you financial aid for the academic year.

Can I sign multiple NLIs?
You can only sign one NLI annually.

Are verbal commitments binding?
While it's common to have a verbal commitment, the NLI program does not recognize them as binding.

Do I have to sign on signing day?
No, signing the NLI is valid at any time.

When I sign an NLI, who am I making an agreement with – the school or the coach?
When you sign an NLI, the letter is an agreement with an institution and not with a coach.

Once I've signed an NLI with an institution, can I sign with anyone else?
Once you sign an NLI, all other institutions are obligated to cease contacting you and your family members. You are required to notify any coach from an NLI institution that you have signed an NLI but contact over an exchange of a greeting is not permitted regardless of the conversation.

If I don't honor my NLI for some reason, then can another school recruit me?
Yes, but only if you have received a complete release or the NLI recruiting ban is lifted if you submit an NLI release request. The NLI recruiting ban is lifted while your NLI release request is pending the signing institution's decision. The NLI recruiting ban is not limited to certain institutions but to all NLI member institutions seeking to recruit you. Note this NLI recruiting ban policy is different from the NCAA Division I notification of transfer or the Division II permission to contact requirements.

Can I get an NLI if I'm a walk on?

No. An institution is strictly prohibited from allowing you to sign an NLI if you are a non-scholarship walk-on. A valid NLI is accompanied by an athletics financial aid award letter, which lists the terms and conditions of the award, including the amount of the financial aid. The athletics financial aid offer must be signed by both the prospective student-athlete and his or her parent or legal guardian. Simply put, there must be an athletics scholarship for an NLI to be valid.

What if I change my mind after I sign?

There could be penalties associated with changing your mind after you sign, so a player should research the current guidelines listed on the NLI site before making a final decision.

What's next?

Receiving a letter of intent is so exciting – and we don't want to deflate your excitement! But we hope that reading this chapter has helped you understand that a letter of intent is serious and should be given proper consideration. Learning all of the details now is your best chance to make the right decision for your baseball career when the time comes.

To further prepare, consider what you read in this chapter and what you already knew. Answer the following questions and do additional research as needed!

1. What information in this chapter was new to you? What additional questions did that new information bring to your mind?

2. How would you explain a letter of intent to a friend or family member? What are the most important points you'd emphasize?

CHAPTER 17

Things to Consider When Deciding on a College

We've given you a lot to think about in this book and a lot of work to do. Everyone follows their path when they pursue playing college ball, and every player has a different set of criteria that will help them make the best choices for their family and their future.

To wrap things up, we want to give you three questions to consider when you're deciding where you want to go to college. Everything we talked about throughout this book falls into one of these categories, but it can be a lot to keep track of, so we hope three simple concepts can help keep you focused and moving forward.

- Can you picture yourself on that college campus?
- Can you see yourself playing on that team?
- Does the school work financially for your family?

We'll provide a summary for each of these considerations just to recap what we covered in the book and remind you of what you need to be focusing on, but it is this simple. We want you to cut through the myths you've heard and grab onto the tactical, practical steps you can begin following now.

Can you picture yourself on that college campus?

Your college experience is going to involve more than playing baseball. It's even going to involve more than attending classes! You have the potential to be living in a completely different part of the country, experiencing a different climate and culture, far away from your family and friends. It's important to ask yourself – and then honestly answer – whether you will be happy on that campus.

Specific questions you should consider include:

- What's the climate (warm weather, cold weather, a lot of rain, etc.) and how do you feel about it? There's nothing wrong with admitting that you'd be miserable in the Midwest because you've never liked the snow. If you know the climate is going to affect how happy you are, don't make a decision that will leave you feeling miserable.
- What kind of city is the college in and how do you feel about it? Does the opportunity to move from a small town to a big city excite you? If so, go ahead and experience that kind of change! But if you know yourself well enough to predict that the city or town the college is located in will cause you to go out too little or too much, consider a location that is a better fit for your needs. You may be going there to play baseball and get a degree, but you will have a life outside of that work and that life will be a big part of your happiness, motivation, and productivity.
- How will you get home for visits and will you be able to maintain the frequency you want? If you choose to live across the country from your home, how often will you be able to come back home? And whatever that frequency is – once a month, just for holidays, etc. – is that financially possible? Sometimes we get so focused on moving away, we forget that college life also means coming home for visits!

When you visit college campuses, pay attention to how you feel. Spend enough time there to see some of the sites, try local restaurants, and get an idea for what the area has to offer.

Can you see yourself playing there?
Unfortunately, getting on a team doesn't guarantee you'll be playing on a team. Before signing your letter of intent, look at the data published by the team and talk to the coach about where you fit on the team roster. Are there multiple other players with your exact skill set that will get played before you will? If so, why does the coach want you on the team? The answer may surprise you, and it will help you decide whether or not the team is right for you.

Hopefully, during the recruitment process, you feel comfortable enough with the coach to honestly ask where you fit on the team. It may seem strange – like you're fishing for a compliment – to ask what makes your specific skills the right investment for the coach. But it isn't an unusual question at all. It demonstrates that you understand the business of baseball and that everyone has a role to play. The coach's answer will help you determine if the role they see for you is a fit for your future.

Does it work financially for your family?
Finally, you have to look past the glamour and prestige of different schools and get down to the important and undeniable details of the cost of your education. If you choose a school that you can't afford, you'll either have to drop out before you're able to graduate or live with the heavy financial burden it places on you and your family. Neither one is a good option, so from the start, ask yourself what you can honestly afford.

When factoring in costs, it isn't just tuition that you have to think about. Be sure to consider:

- Tuition (after scholarships are applied)
- Educational materials (books, computer, etc.)
- Cost of living (room and board, food, transportation, etc.)
- Travel (visits home)

When you add financial considerations to your calculations, you may find that choosing a school becomes a much easier decision. Some schools may be ruled out because they are just too expensive. Other schools that you thought were too expensive may seem more affordable once you see the real numbers. Plotting out educational costs in detail will help you override any pre-conceived notions and make the best possible financial decision.

Like every chapter in this book, we're wrapping things up by encouraging you to complete a few exercises. We want you to do more than just think about the information we've shared. We want you to do the work and put it into action. Answering the following questions and the questions at the end of each chapter in the book will help you do just that.

What's next?

Congratulations! You made it to the end of the book. If you've been working through the material chapter by chapter, you already have a great start to the different things you need to work on. Now is your opportunity to go back through your work and clarify your to-do list.

1. Consider the three questions asked in this chapter.
   - Can you picture yourself on that college campus?
   - Can you see yourself playing on that team?
   - Does the school work financially for your family?

   Discuss the answers with your family and write them down. It's okay if you don't have every answer yet because writing out the answers you do have will help you clarify what additional information you still need.

2. Go back to the beginning of this book and make sure you completed each chapter exercise! You may have skipped a few because of timing or because you needed to do additional research, so now is the time to double back and complete the steps you skipped.

End Notes

ncaa.org[i]

Made in the USA
Middletown, DE
27 November 2021